"He told them another parable: 'The kingdom of heaven is like a mustard seed, which a man took and planted in his field...'" (Matthew 13:31).

The Mustard Seed Associates team seeks to enable followers of Jesus– especially those who are innovators and unsatisfied with 'status quo' faith– to a counter cultural way of life. We encourage people to create new and innovative forms of whole life faith that advance God's purposes locally and globally and engage tomorrow's challenges. We want to create processes and offer resources that ignite people's creativity and inspire them to live as agents of faith—a faith that is more culturally subversive and revolutionary than we can fully understand or imagine.

ADDITIONAL MSA RESOURCES

PUBLICATIONS

Waiting for the Light: An Advent Devotional, compiled by Susan Wade, Ricci Kilmer & Christine Sine
Return to Our Senses: Reimagining How We Pray, by Christine Sine
To Garden with God, by Christine Sine
To Garden with God: Color Edition, by Christine Sine
Light for the Journey: Morning and Evening Prayers for Living into God's Word, by Christine Sine
GodSpace: Time for Peace in the Rhythms of Life, by Christine Sine
Living On Purpose: Finding God's Best for Your Life, by Christine and Tom Sine
The New Conspirators, by Tom Sine

E-BOOKS

Celebrating the Joy of Easter, by Christine Sine
Turbulent Times, Ready or Not!, by Tom Sine
Shalom and the Wholeness of God, by Christine Sine
Justice at the Table, by Ricci Kilmer

To Garden With God (.PDF, .MOBI, .ePUB Versions)
Waiting for the Light: An Advent Devotional (PDF Version)
Waiting for the Light: An Advent Devotional (Kindle Version)
A Journey into Wholeness: a Lenten Journey (PDF Version)

ADDITIONAL RESOURCES

Prayer Cards
Gardener's Soap
Study Guide

All resources (including video and audio resources, tickets to MSA events, study guides and links to blogs) can be accessed and ordered at http://msaimagine.org/resources.

A Journey
Into Wholeness

-Soul Travel From Lent To Easter-

COMPILED BY CHRISTINE SINE,
KRISTIN CARROCCINO, AND RICCI KILMER

Unless otherwise noted, quotations are taken from THE HOLY BIBLE: NEW INTERNATIONAL VERSION®. NIV®. Copyright © 1973, 1978, 1984 by Biblica. Used by permission of Biblica. All rights reserved worldwide.

Scripture quotations marked TNIV are taken from THE HOLY BIBLE, TODAY'S NEW INTERNATIONAL VERSION®. Copyright © 2001, 2005 by Biblica®. Used by permission of Biblica®. All rights reserved worldwide. "TNIV" and "Today's New International Version" are trademarks registered in the United States Patent and Trademark Office by Biblica. Use of either trademark requires the permission of Biblica.

Scripture quotations marked NLT are taken from THE HOLY BIBLE, NEW LIVING TRANSLATION®. Copyright © 1996, 2004. Used by permission of Tyndale House Publishers, Wheaton, IL 60189. All rights reserved.

Scripture quotations marked Phillips are taken from THE NEW TESTAMENT IN MODERN ENGLISH®. Copyright © 1962. Used by permission of HarperCollins.

ISBN: 978-0615937823

Cover Credits: Kristin Carroccino

DEDICATION

To all who seek to journey with Jesus
towards a deeper faith and a more centered life.

TABLE OF CONTENTS

About the Compilers

Christine Sine is the Executive Director of Mustard Seed Associates. She trained as a physician in Australia and developed the medical ministry for Mercy Ships. She now speaks on issues relating to changing our timestyles and lifestyles to develop a more spiritual rhythm for life. She has authored several books including *Return to Our Senses: Reimagining How We Pray*; *Godspace: Time for Peace in the Rhythms of Life*; and *Tales of a Seasick Doctor*. Christine blogs at http://godspace-msa.com. Christine contributed the introductory sections, litanies, blog posts and resources for this book.

Kristin Carroccino is a writer and photographer and volunteer for Mustard Seed Associates. She lives in Seattle with her husband Michael and two young children. More of her writing can be found at http://boatswithoutoars.blogspot.com, which is a record of a cross-country journey studying Episcopal churches in the summer of 2012. As well as her blog post, she contributed the wonderful cover design and used her editorial skills to refine and strengthen the publication.

Ricci Kilmer lives with her husband and three children in Seattle, Washington. For some time she has been interested in combining faith with the practicality of daily life. In 2010 she integrated her love of food and desire for justice into a resource entitled Justice at the Table. Ricci headed up the mammoth task of gathering reflections from the blog, tracking down authors to ensure that their biographical information was current and providing the initial formatting and design for the book.

ACKNOWLEDGEMENTS

This has been a fun project to work on. Revisiting what people have posted on godspace-msa.com as Lenten reflections in the last few years has stimulated and encouraged all of us who have worked on this book.

We want to thank those faithful bloggers who contribute regularly to Godspace. Their contributions, whether published in this book or not, enrich and encourage all of us as we walk together towards God's eternal world. We are very aware that these reflections come from people's hearts and are grateful for the time and effort that goes into their production. We are especially grateful to those whose reflections do appear in *A Journey into Wholeness*. Thank you for your gracious help in rewriting dated material, and for your patience with us as we nagged you for biographical information and citations.

A special thank you to Kari Rauh who spent many hours reading, editing and formatting the book for publication. Without her help it would never have been published.

I also want to thank my collaborators in this project, Kristin Carroccino and Ricci Kilmer, whose commitment and enthusiasm endured through long hours of compilation and editing. Kristin has gone the extra mile photographing the image for the cover over and over until we were all satisfied with it. The cross in this photo is a very special one created by Kayra Inslee at one of our prayer retreats. She wove the circle from woven tree roots and I hung tillandsia (air plants) on it to symbolize life in barren places. The rocks are ones I have collected as memories of special events and places.

Finally I want to thank the Mustard Seed Associates team – my husband Tom Sine, Andy Wade and Cindy Todd – whose dedication to all we do at MSA has helped to bring this project to completion.

BEGINNING

A Journey into Lent

Lent is the season before Easter that commemorates the forty days Jesus spent in the wilderness in preparation for his ministry. This season invites us to contemplate our own Christian journey and consider the disciplines we should practice to guide us towards God's wholeness. It is a time to reflect on how we can deepen our relationship to God as we represent and meet with Christ through our words and action.

Many of us are unfamiliar with the practice of Lent, though its observance is gaining popularity in a wide variety of churches, from Baptist to Pentecostal. Those of us who do acknowledge it tend to think of Lent as a time to give up a non-essential food item like chocolate or to cut back on activities like watching TV. Some of us fast for a day or two and get a warm glow of satisfaction because of our sacrifice, but these observances make little (if any) difference to the ongoing journey of our lives.

Lent is not really about sacrifice or deprivation. In the early church, this was a time of preparation for those about to be baptized. Today it is more often regarded as a season of soul-searching and repentance for all Christians as a preparation for the joy and celebration of Easter. Unfortunately our soul searching is often as perfunctory as our sacrifices. We spend a little more time reading the Bible and praying. Some of us spend a few hours working with a local mission, but otherwise our lives are unchanged. And after Easter, there is very little to show for our commitment.

Traditionally, Lent is marked by penitential prayer, fasting, and almsgiving. Some churches still observe a rigid schedule of fasting often on Fridays, especially giving up of meat, alcohol, sweets, and other types of food. Other traditions do not place as great an emphasis on fasting, but focus on charitable deeds (especially helping those in physical need with food and clothing) or simply the giving of money to charities. Most Christian churches that observe Lent see it as a time for penitential prayer, repenting for failures and sin as a way to focus on the need for God's grace. It is really a preparation to celebrate God's marvelous redemption at Easter, and the resurrected life that we live-and hope for-as Christians.

I love the way that Theresa Ip Froehlich explains the place of fasting during Lent:

> Giving up something is an expression of fasting, but to divorce fasting from mourning is to miss the first Beatitude in Jesus' Sermon on the Mount. "Blessed are the poor in spirit, for theirs is the kingdom of heaven" (Mt. 5:3). Perhaps the place to begin isn't with which creature comforts, addictive appetites, or innocuous idolatries we choose to abstain from for a limited period of time. The place to begin is to take to heart our spiritual bankruptcy, our propensity to love the little idols more than we love God, and our unbelief about the transformative power of God's Spirit. When we begin with this, our hands will be pried open to receive what God has to give us. We will no longer approach God as the resourceful Giver who brings the gift of abstinence. Instead we will approach him as beggars. "Blessed are those who mourn, for they will be comforted" (Mt. 5:4).[1]

Interestingly, the concept of spring-cleaning emerged from the practice of Lent. This was the time of year when one cleaned house—first physically and then spiritually. The holistic intention behind this practice informs our Lenten practice. What we "sweep out" or give up should be more than food: this is the time to give up our busyness and sweep out the destructive habits that keep us focused on ourselves and our own selfish desires in order to focus on the truly important things of God. It is a good time to give up social events and engagements that keep us busy and distract us from the need to uncover our brokenness so that we can find forgiveness and healing. The time we free up can be used for special prayers and Bible readings that help us to uncover the broken areas of our lives. Or they can be used for spiritual retreats and involvement in local or overseas mission that enables us to focus beyond ourselves and onto our responsibility to those who are hurting and in need. Often it is in reaching out to other broken and disabled people that we find the road to our healing.

This year during Lent, we invite you to join us on a journey with Jesus to the cross and beyond, using *A Journey Into Wholeness* as a guide. This resource is designed to take you on a weekly journey into different aspects of the brokenness of God's world so that you can become an instrument of God's healing and restoration. Our journey will begin with a few days of meditations preparing us for Lent, which begins on Ash Wednesday, and will conclude with Holy Week and Easter Sunday, reminding us that the crucifixion was not an end but a beginning as we celebrate the emergence of God's gift of new life to our world through the resurrection. Each week, themes will change, and you will be invited to take time each day to deepen your relationship with God during the season of Lent. Many of the reflections in this guide are taken from an annual Lenten blog series on my blog http://godspace-msa.com. Contributors come from around the globe providing richly diverse and often provocative viewpoints. Even their grammar, punctuation and spelling varies. Out of respect for each author's unique style and country of origin, punctuation and spelling were kept in accordance with how they appeared in their original posting.

A JOURNEY WITH JESUS

The idea of journeying is fundamental to the Christian faith. From the time that God extended an invitation to Abraham and Sarah to "leave your native country, your relatives, and your father's family and go to the land that I will show you," (Gen. 12:1), people of faith have journeyed away from their old lives and the cultures in which they grew up (both physically and spiritually) toward a deeper understanding of God and God's purposes. In the Middle Ages, Christians were encouraged to make pilgrimages to special holy places called shrines. It was believed that if you prayed at these shrines you might be forgiven for your sins and have a better chance of going to heaven. Others went to shrines hoping to be cured from an illness.

Journeying, or in Latin *peregrinatio*, from which we get the English word "pilgrimage," was also essential to Celtic Christianity, which spread throughout Europe in the 4th to 8th centuries. Believers often left home and loved ones with no specific physical destination in mind, but rather to go on an inner journey to find Christ. They believed their home was not this world, but the heavenly Jerusalem, toward which all of life moves us. They saw themselves as "guests of the world." From the perspective of these early believers, every experience encountered and every activity undertaken on the way was an opportunity to meet or to represent Christ.

As an expression of their devotion, early Christian pilgrims to Jerusalem retraced Jesus' route as he carried his cross to his death. By the sixteenth century, this pilgrimage route through Jerusalem was called the *Via Dolorosa*, or the Way of Sorrow. Along the Way, certain points on the journey (stations) were associated with specific events recounted or implied in the Gospel accounts. There are presently fourteen Stations of the Cross on the *Via Dolorosa*, some with chapels or places to pray and meditate. Today churches of all traditions have rediscovered their significance and invite people from their community to walk the stations with Jesus. They may not necessarily make a physical journey to Jerusalem, but create a virtual experience of Jesus' final walk, often setting up the stations around the church sanctuary or another facility.

The horror of Christ's crucifixion reaches deep into our souls. As I walk with Jesus along this virtual *Via Dolorosa*, I am often overwhelmed by memories of when I too felt abandoned and alone. Knowing in those moments that Christ endured more pain and suffering than I can ever imagine powerfully opens a door in the midst of my darkness and provides a way for me to emerge into new life.

Walking with Jesus through the agonies of his final journey is an incredible opportunity for us to express the pain and grief we have suffered over the past year. In the process, we find the healing that only comes through such intimate identification with Christ.

I find that Good Friday is a time when people are looking for prayers to pray and reflections to meditate on. The following prayer is one I wrote as a blog post specifically for Good Friday while reflecting on the incredible depth of Jesus' suffering. Other prayers are available on Godspace.

JESUS, OUR ADVOCATE

Jesus, our advocate,
In the darkness of Gethsemane
You wept for us.
Shedding tears of blood,
You shared our pain.
Jesus our redeemer,
On the way to the Cross
You suffered for us.
Tortured, spat upon and despised,
You carried our burdens.
Jesus our Saviour,
On the hill of Calvary
You died for us.
Crucified and hung upon a tree,
You released us into freedom.
Son of the living God,
Redeemer, Saviour, Advocate,
Through the journey of suffering,
In the place of darkness,
You overcame death forever,
And gave us new life.
Amen.

A JOURNEY INTO WHOLENESS

At the center of God's vision for the future is a wonderful dream of an eternal world in which all of creation is restored to the wholeness and harmony of relationships. It is this new world, not the cross, which is the end of our journey. God looks forward to the day when all people are restored physically, emotionally, and spiritually to be a part of a new heaven and a new earth in which all creation finds completion and fulfillment. To be a disciple of Christ means to grab hold of this vision and make it the destination for our life's journey. We deliberately choose to lay down our own self-centered lives and consciously live each moment journeying towards God's presence and towards a life that is fully integrated with God's will for restoration and wholeness. The Holy Spirit is constantly at work in us, breaking down the barriers that distort our ability to lead a life that is fully integrated with God's purposes.

According to Henri Nouwen, "Discipline is the creation of boundaries that keep time and space open for God—a time and place where God's gracious presence can be acknowledged and responded to."[2] Lent is a special season for developing this type of discipline.

When humankind was expelled from the Garden of Eden and separated from God, it was not just our relationship to God that was distorted and broken. Our relationship to each other, our stewardship of the earth, and even our inner harmony were all broken and distorted by sin. Our journey through Lent toward the cross should encourage us to confront all these areas of brokenness and lead us to a place of healing and wholeness.

Lent is far more than a journey out of brokenness, however. At the heart of the biblical story is not the sinfulness of humankind but the love and forgiveness of God. As we journey toward the cross we are not meant to wallow in our sin even though we desperately need to acknowledge it and seek repentance and forgiveness. The reason we focus on our brokenness and need for repentance is so that we can be healed and enabled to become the people that God intends us to be: people who live and work together in harmony and mutual trust, caring for creation and relating intimately to our loving Creator.

A JOURNEY FROM ASH WEDNESDAY TO GOOD FRIDAY

Lent begins with Ash Wednesday and ends with Good Friday, days which mark the beginning and ending of an important life journey as we walk with Jesus through the final days of his life to his crucifixion.

Ash Wednesday is a day for repentance, intended to cleanse the soul before the Lenten fast. Roman Catholic, Anglican, and other denominations hold special services on this day at which worshippers are marked with ashes as a symbol of death, and a sign of penitence and mortality. Often the ashes are produced by burning the Palm Sunday crosses from the previous year. As each participant is marked, the minister or priest says: "Remember you are dust and

5

unto dust you shall return," or a similar phrase based on God's words to Adam in Genesis 3:19. At some churches, worshippers leave with the mark still on their forehead so that they carry the sign of the cross out into the world. At others, the service ends with the ashes being washed off as a sign that the participants have been cleansed of their sins.

Good Friday commemorates the crucifixion and Jesus' final sacrifice for the redemption of our world. The cross is not meant to be the focus of our mourning and fasting during Lent, however. We mourn and fast not because we are heading to the cross but because we want to shed all the obstacles that keep us from living an intimate walk with God.

I want to become all that God intends me to be. I want to leave behind all that hinders me from becoming that person. I want to thirst for righteousness and hunger for justice rather than for water and food. It is not an easy journey, but then neither was Jesus' journey through the cross to resurrection.

A JOURNEY INTO SABBATH REST FOR ALL

A couple of months ago I came across this quote from Thomas Merton's *Seasons of Celebration:*

> God's people first came into existence when the children of Israel were delivered from slavery in Egypt and called out into the desert to be educated in freedom, to learn how to live with no other master but God himself.[3]

I could not help but think of it as I was rereading Dorothy Bass's chapter on Sabbath in *Practicing Our Faith.*[4] She talks about the fact that Sabbath had two meanings for the Hebrews. The Exodus commandment to remember the Sabbath is grounded in the creation story when God rested in appreciated and satisfaction of all creation. In the Deuteronomy account Sabbath observance is tied to the experience of a people newly released from bondage.

Slaves cannot take a day off; free people can. Thus, Sabbath rest is a recurring testimony against the drudgery of slavery. Together, these two renderings of the Sabbath commandment summarize the most fundamental stories and beliefs of the Hebrew Scriptures: creation and exodus, humanity in God's image and a people liberated from captivity. One emphasizes holiness, the other social justice. Sabbath crystallizes the Torah's portrait of who God is and what human beings are most fully meant to be.

The journey through Lent is a journey into the freedoms of Sabbath, not just for ourselves, but for all humankind. To undertake this journey, however, we must first learn to rest in the freedom of gratitude and appreciation. So many of our efforts throughout the week and the year are focused on striving for more – more money, more success, more stuff- and few of us ever take the time to be grateful. We are so easily caught up in the same forces that motivate people who are not followers of Jesus. Moving into this freedom requires inward reflection and examination of our motives and the forces that drive us.

Another purpose of Lent is to become dissatisfied with our own bondage and the bondage of others. It is about looking for ways to bring freedom and liberation not just for ourselves but for all who live in the bondage of poverty, imprisonment, servitude or injustice. For millions of workers, long Sunday hours for rest and worship may be impossible within the current system. People who know the Sabbath pattern of creation, liberation and resurrection nurture a dissatisfaction with this system and work for change.

Christians started to celebrate Sunday (the eighth day) rather than Saturday (seventh day in the Jewish week) as the Sabbath day because they believed that with the resurrection of Christ the future of God had burst into the present world. Easter Sunday was the fulfillment of the Old Testament Sabbath principle. Thus. the freedom we work towards during Lent is the freedom of liberation from slavery – not just for ourselves but for all humankind.

So how do we follow Jesus toward the Cross and ensure that this Easter something of God's Sabbath rest comes not just into our own lives but into the lives of all who are in pain or suffering in our world?

A JOURNEY BEYOND EASTER SUNDAY INTO GOD'S RESURRECTION WORLD

Lent is about looking beyond the cross to life in God's kingdom. Asking myself what I still need to repent of and what needs to be transformed in my life so that I can be an effective citizen of God's eternal world are probably the most important questions of Lent. That is why this study guide does not stop with Good Friday and the crucifixion but prompts us to walk with Jesus through the tomb to Easter Sunday.

For many of us, Easter Sunday represents the culmination of our faith, the day for which all of us have waited, hoped and longed. This is in many ways the end of our journey, but it is not the end of our story. In fact, it is just the beginning. Easter isn't just a single day; it is a whole season. How could we possibly celebrate the wonder of God's new world which was ushered in by the resurrection in a single day? And how can we possibly confine the practice of this incredible event to a short church service?

In the liturgical calendar the Easter season extends until Pentecost, but for those of us who have entered God's new world, Easter is the celebration of the rest of our lives. We are called to practice resurrection, to go out and not just shout about the new life we have in Christ but to live it. Jesus' resurrection transformed his disciples. They left homes and families and jobs to live radically different lives. They sold their property and shared it with others. They looked after the sick and cared for the marginalized. This small band of disciples became a worldwide movement that still transforms lives today. The goal of this guide is to help us, like that small band of early believers, to consider our lives, take the time to be immersed in the world around us, and be renewed and transformed to live as resurrection people in God's kingdom in the here and now.

ENTER THE WEEKLY JOURNEY

Over the six weeks of Lent as we journey with Christ toward the cross, we want to examine areas of brokenness in our lives and in the world and explore how we can move closer to God and more effectively be God's hands of healing and wholeness. Our journey will begin with an exploration of the barriers within ourselves that resist God's will: selfishness, fear, feelings of abandonment and our inability to trust that God really loves us all separate us from God and the life that God wants for us.

In the second and third weeks, we will confront some of the barriers that separate us from other human beings: a lack of forgiveness, the desire to control, greed, and an indifference to the suffering of others all distort our relationships to those with whom we share this planet. In the fourth week, we will explore barriers that separate us from God's creation: lack of proper stewardship, over-consumption and a lack of respect for what God has made all destroy our relationship to God's creation. In the fifth week of Lent, we will confront some of the barriers that isolate us from other parts of God's family because of lack of unity between believers with different theological perspectives. Independence, the desire to "do it my way," and the lack of unity with fellow believers are all barriers to a mature relationship with God. Holy week, the last week of Lent, will focus on Jesus' own walk toward the cross and the brokenness he willing endured to set us free.

It is not surprising that in a culture like ours (one that craves comfort and ease), few people practice fasting and self-sacrifice during Lent anymore. Deliberately walking with Christ towards the Cross is very costly. In fact, it demands our whole life.

We pray that this year will be different. As we journey this year towards the Cross, may we walk towards a deeper commitment to God. In the words of the apostle Paul,

> *Since we are surrounded by such a great cloud of witnesses, let us throw off everything that hinders and the sin that so easily entangles, and let us run with perseverance the race marked out for us. Let us fix our eyes on Jesus, the author and perfecter of our faith, who for the joy set before him endured the cross, scorning its shame, and sat down at the right hand of the throne of God. Consider him who endured such opposition from sinful men, so that you will not grow weary and lose heart.* (Heb. 12:1-3)

As you prepare for this Lenten season together, there are several disciplines to consider that will facilitate your journey.

This journey is not meant to be traveled alone. Plan to begin each week with a group meeting with a spouse or friends. Look at your schedule for the six weeks of Lent. What do you need to give up over this period to make weekly meetings possible? These times together are an important part of your journey. Plan a simple (soup and bread) meal as part of your community discipline. Give a different person responsibility for the meal each week. Allow time to discuss your struggles and plan your week's activities. Pray for each other and for those who are less fortunate in our world.

Find an Ash Wednesday service to attend as the first act of your Lenten journey. The imposition of ashes is a great way to start our Lenten journey as it reminds us of the need we all have for repentance and forgiveness. Attend the service with your small group or friends. Afterwards, spend time reflecting on the experience and how it has affected your view of Lent. Are there areas in your life that God has prompted you to repent of publicly? Did God challenge you to make specific commitments for the entire duration of the Lenten season?

Set aside time each day during Lent for solitary reflection. Buy a new journal, specifically to reflect on your Lenten journey. Each day read through the Scripture passages designated for the week in the *Book of Common Prayer* or *Revised Common Lectionary*.[5] Which verse stands out for you? Read this verse aloud several times. Then spend time in quiet reflection. What is God saying to you through this verse? Write down any reflections, thoughts, and prayers that come out of your time. This same practice of observation and reflection can be applied to other words we read during the day.

Use the weekly litanies as a way to focus. The prayers and litanies in each section are designed not just to be used in as a way to focus during your weekly meetings. They are intended as daily reminders of our commitment during this season. You may like to write the week's prayer, or part of it, on a card that you carry with you each day. On the same card, write down what you intend to do as your Lenten discipline for that week. Read through the litany and your commitment each morning and spend time reflecting on what that could look like in the day that is coming. Some of the litanies provide images of God's dream for a transformed world. Others suggest places in which we need to recognize our own brokenness and repent.

Following Jesus towards the Cross is a serious business that requires discipline and commitment. We hope that you will accept the invitation to journey with us and find another part of the wholeness God intends for us, and for our world.

Preparing for Lent:

Journey with Jesus Toward the Cross

Enter the Journey

Journeys don't just happen. To be successful they need careful preparation. We must decide what to take, who our companions will be, where we will meet and what we will do together. Above all we must count the cost of our decision. This journey into Lent and beyond is no exception. It does no good to make a commitment to walk with Jesus through the season of Lent and then bail out.

The beginning of Lent in the Western church is Ash Wednesday, 46 days before Easter. It derives its name from the practice of placing ashes, usually in the shape of a cross, on the foreheads of adherents as a reminder of human mortality and as a sign of mourning and repentance to God. Typically, the ashes used are gathered from the burning of palms from the previous year's Palm Sunday.

The days leading up to Ash Wednesday are meant to prepare us for this important journey into wholeness. If possible, plan your first meeting for the Sunday before Ash Wednesday so that you can talk about your expectations of this journey together.

Shrove Tuesday is the day before Ash Wednesday. "Shrove" is the past tense of the word "shrive," which means to hear a confession, assign penance, and absolve from sin. Shrove Tuesday is a reminder that we are entering a season of penance.

Shrove Tuesday is also known as Fat Tuesday or Mardi Gras (French for Fat Tuesday). In Italy, Fat Tuesday is known as *carnevale,* or "goodbye to meat," from which we get our English word *carnival.* Traditionally people held one last rich feast, using up perishables like eggs, butter and milk before the fast of Lent began. Now in some places, like New Orleans, this has become a huge celebration that really has nothing to do with the beginning of Lent and certainly nothing to do with fasting. For many however this is still a significant day. Churches hold pancake suppers, often as a way to reach out to their neighbours.

For Eastern Orthodox Christians the fast begins at the beginning of the week. Clean Monday, the Monday before Ash Wednesday, is the first day of Great Lent. It is a reminder that we should begin Lent with good intentions and a desire to clean our spiritual house. It is a day of strict fasting for Eastern Catholics and Orthodox, including abstinence not only from meat but from eggs and dairy products as well.

- Plan a meal together. Get each person to answer the question: What are your hopes and expectations for this journey? If possible have each person write down their expectations on a paper that can kept in this book until Easter Sunday when they can be read aloud again with a brief description of what has been accomplished.
- Decide which daily readings you want to use in conjunction with the reflections in this book. There is a fairly extensive list in the resources at the end of the book to choose from or you may have another setting of readings you might like to use.
- If you have time, watch the movie *Chocolat* together.

A Litany for Ash Wednesday

We have chosen to fast,
Not with ashes but with actions,
Not with sackcloth but in sharing,
Not in thoughts but in deeds.
We will give up our abundance,
To share our food with the hungry.
We will give up our comfort,
To provide homes for the destitute.
We will give up our fashions,
To see the naked clothed.
We will share where others hoard,
And free where others oppress.
We will heal where others harm.
Then God's light will break out on us,
God's healing will quickly appear.
God will guide us always.
God's righteousness will go before us,
And we will find our joy in the Lord.
We will be like a well-watered garden,
And will be called repairers of broken walls.
Together we will feast at God's banquet table.
And live in God's eternal world forever.
Amen.

MONDAY

"Lenten Fasting; Easter Feasting"
Rachel Stone

I'm not sure what the actual stats were, but it sure seemed like most of the kids in my high school were Catholic. When I started going there as an eighth grader, everyone (it seemed) was busy making their confirmations. On Ash Wednesday, lots of people went around with ashes marked on their foreheads.

And while I'm pretty sure it wasn't constitutional or whatever, somehow it seems that the school lunches on Fridays during Lent tended toward the fish stick and pizza variety and away from the *fleisch* products. Could it have been so? I can't be sure, but I definitely remember people "giving up" various things–chocolate, swearing, soda–for Lent.

I must admit, I always felt a little left out as one of the few Protestant-y type Christians. Because I don't how much my A Beka curriculum told me that the Catholic Church was BAD, I found all that liturgy and incense and images and ashes and abnegation attractive; a welcome change from the excessively inward "is your heart right with God?" kind of thing. I could always see–can still see– how holding a cross and a circle of beads might help one's mind stay on one's prayers.

But it wasn't until after college, I think, that I started to see some of my fellow evangelical-type Christians practicing Lent in the more modern style of "giving something up." (Orthodox Christians still go vegan for Lent; traditionally, Lenten fasts involved limiting meals to one a day and fasting from various animal products. Hence, Mardi Gras-type celebrations are called Carnival in Latin America: "farewell, medium-well!")

Some Christians see the tradition of Lent–beginning with Ash Wednesday and ending forty days later, on Easter Sunday–as a way of "fasting while the bridegroom is taken." Others see it as a way of participating in Jesus' 40 days of desert temptation. In any case, practicing some kind of fasting during Lent is definitely no longer a 'Catholic' thing. What's its appeal?

1. Lenten Fasting Makes Outward and Visible Stuff That Is Otherwise Just In Your Head

A vintage (circa 1960) Christianity Today article put it this way:

> Lent can become a time when material things are put again in their proper secondary position; when we see in the spiritual the unconquerable forces of life. It can become a time of self-examination, when we reflect upon our present position in the pilgrimage and check our directions. It can become a time of personal readjustment, not through mental resolutions to do better but through yielding ourselves afresh to the God who demands to be obeyed. And it can become a time when, by following the battered path to Calvary, we identify ourselves once again with the Saviour who makes all things new.[6]

And in an NPR interview, the inimitable Anne Lamott said: "Ash Wednesday, to me, is about as plain as it gets — we come from ashes and return to ashes, and yet there is something, as the poets have often said, that remains standing when we're gone."[7]

Hence Facebook, online, and other media-fasts. Not "I should spend less time doing this or more time doing that," but a firm resolution to do so. Can this be 'legalism'? Sure. Can it just be a Good and Healthy Discipline? Absolutely.

2. Lenten Fasting Gives You a Good Reason to Say No To Good Things

Andrew Santella wrote the following for Slate a few years back:

> Perhaps it's the things that made Lent hard to take as a Catholic kid —the solemnity, the self-denial, the disappearance of hot dogs from the lunchroom—that account most for the season's broadening appeal. I was schooled to see Lent as a time apart, a respite from the daily pursuit of self-gratification.[8]

And likewise Lauren Winner: "In sated and overfed America [...] fasting teaches us that we are not utterly subject to our bodily desires."[9]

Greediness is tiring. A season of voluntary simplicity is–or can be–one way of taking a kind of rest. Also, it can be a way of expressing solidarity with those whose simplicity is not-so-voluntary.

3. Lenten Fasting Provides a Counterpoint To Easter Feasting

My favorite Episcopalian priest I've never met, Robert Farrar Capon, exalts the rhythm of festal/ferial as a splendid way of ordering our appetites. Because really, how much better is Easter Dinner–how much sweeter a sacramental celebrating that Joy of Joys–when you have prepared for it by fasting?
The sensation I always remember in this regard is how incredibly tasty a nasty freeze-dried meal by the fire with friends can taste when you've been hiking up and over mountains all day on nothing but water and GORP–a sweet nectar/ sore need dynamic.

Again, Anne Lamott, on the breaking of the Lenten fast–i.e., Easter Sunday:

> I'm going to go to my little church, and we will have a huge crowd of about 60 people. And I will cry a little bit ... out of joy, and then I will go home, and I will have 25 people — 15 relatives and about 10 riffraff, i.e., my closest friends — and we will sit down and we will eat, the most sacred thing we do.[10]

Amen.
Even though I want to fast, I'm not quite sure what form that will take for me/ us this year.
What is your take on Lenten fasting? Will you fast this Lent? How?

Rachel Marie Stone is the author of Eat With Joy: Redeeming God's Gift of Food *(InterVarsity Press, 2013) and of the forthcoming book about Jesus for children,* The Unexpected Way *(Olive Branch Books, 2014). Her writing has appeared in* Christianity Today, Books & Culture, The Christian Century, RELEVANT, Prism, *and* The Huffington Post *among others, and she has contributed essays to several collected volumes. She lives in Malawi, Africa, where she teaches writing at Zomba Theological College.*

TUESDAY

"Introspection and Lent"
Gil George

I have a lot of friends who are part of formal liturgical traditions that practice Lent. Even in some of the churches in the Yearly Meeting I am a part of there are discussions of Lent, and some even celebrate it to one degree or another. I am quite frequently invited to participate in Lenten observances or reflections, and this essay is my attempt to explain why I struggle with how to participate in this conversation, not only as a Quaker, but as the person God created me to be.

Introspection is an ongoing process that is an integral part of a close relationship. My wife and I regularly discuss how things are going in our marriage relationship; we don't just talk about how things are for a brief season every year. In the same way my relationship with God has times of introspection that occur on a regular basis in order for us to hear how we each perceive the other and ourselves to be doing in the relationship. These times are sometimes daily and sometimes weekly, but that is about as long as I can go without holding my life in the light of the Holy Spirit.

When I get formal and address things in a formal manner that is my way of putting distance between me and others, including God. This is definitely not a universal thing and I realize it, but this is the way my mind operates. This desire for intimacy in my daily walk is one of the main reasons that the Quaker church has been so helpful for my journey with God.

I am a Myers-Briggs type ESFP. My focus is on the immediate and I desire to live fully into the now. If there is cause to celebrate I am not going to care about what the calendar says, I am going to throw a party. If there is cause to grieve, I will mourn with my whole heart even if the calendar says it is party time. Life never has been neat enough for me to be able to assign times of mourning or rejoicing however, there always seems to be sorrow alongside the joy and joy alongside the sorrow. In many ways it has become impossible for me to separate the two, every day is Lent and Easter. I wait for Christ to come and redeem me and Christ has already come. I feel the death embodied in my brokenness and I am resurrected every day.

In the liturgical traditions a majority of the year (33-34 weeks) is spent in what is called "Ordinary Time," and this is where I live. I have a deep love and appreciation for the insights and openings that come from the faithful practices of mundane life. From preparing meals and washing dishes to the daily "Dear God time" prayers as I tuck my daughter in to bed I find my connection to God and life deepen. As I fold the warm clothes after pulling them out of the drier and drape towels over my daughter's head or have a "sock fight" in which we throw socks at each other I feel the love and presence of God. I occasionally wake up as tired as when I went to bed, and on most days I look in the mirror and wonder if I am ever going to be able to lose the weight. When the bumps, bruises, fears and crises of everyday life come, those are ministers of the ordinary as well, drawing me daily into the arms of the Spirit who I cling to as a Mama. She wraps her arms around me and daily mourns my deepest wounds with sighs that reach the deepest, darkest corners of my being, bringing light and healing.

May your Lenten season be blessed and may you find Christ in the ordinary.

Gil George is a Christ-centered Quaker who is part of the Northwest Yearly Meeting. He has been released for ministry as the Senior Pastor of Clackamas Park Friends Church and just graduated from George Fox Evangelical Seminary. He lives in Washington with his wife Mel and young daughter, Grace. He blogs at extrovertedquaker.wordpress.com.

ASH WEDNESDAY

"Thank God for Lent"
Theresa Ip Froehlich

The lights in the sanctuary were dimmed.

As the worshippers arrived, each one went forward to light a candle and placed it in the box filled with sand. The flickering flames from the candles seemed exceptionally bright against the background of dimmed lights.

At the end of the worship time, we went forward to have the ashes placed on our foreheads. As the ministers and the elders made the sign of the cross on our foreheads, they said, "Dust you are, and to dust you will return."

This was the Ash Wednesday worship service at a large Presbyterian Church, marking the beginning of Lent. Having grown up a Roman Catholic, I am very familiar with the practice of the imposition of ashes. Yet, this time, after having followed Jesus Christ for 34 years, I connected with the meaning of the ashes at a much deeper level.

As a young child, I used to like to a visit a Roman Catholic cemetery near my grandparents' home to look at the beautiful statues of cherubim on the graves. The gate to the cemetery was inscribed with those same words from Genesis 3:19, "Dust thou art, and to dust thou shall return." In my young mind, I could only think of how the earth had forever separated my grandparents from me and how powerless I was to change that fact.

Contemplating on mortality is a good thing.

At this annual opportunity at Lent to remember my status as mere mortals, I am also able to refocus on God as the Everlasting and Almighty One. The imposition of ashes on my forehead once again reminds me that I am a creature and God is my Creator, that I am finite while God is infinite, and that I am mortal while God is immortal.

Being creaturely, finite, and mortal also calls for a particular relationship with and response to God. Brian Doerksen, in his song "Return To Me" sums it up powerfully and succinctly:

> From the ancient days until today
> I have inspired prophets and poets
> And at the heart of every message
> Are these three words
> 'Return to me'
> I am Your creator; return to me
> I am Your Redeemer....Your Father; return to me
> I am Your husband; return to me.[11]

The three words "Return to me" form the short love letter God writes to each one of us. The Hebrew word for repentance is "shuv," which literally means "making a U-turn." God our Heavenly Father created us, loves us, and wants us to enjoy a close relationship with him. Our tendency to wander away from him and to set ourselves up as the god-in-charge is also the reason we need at least an annual reminder of who we are: that we are mere mortals.

Repenting of my delusion about my own godlike status, my inflated sense of self-importance, and my forgetfulness about God as the Almighty One, I come face to face with my arrogance, my autonomy, my self-absorption, and my powerlessness.

And I thank God for Lent, especially for the ashes on Ash Wednesday which remind me "the poor in spirit" and those who "mourn [for our sins]" are the blessed ones. The prophet Jeremiah calls for repentance with these words, "O daughter of my people, gird on sackcloth, roll in ashes" (Jeremiah 6:26). And Job, the great sufferer, says to God, "I know you can do all things; no plan of yours can be thwarted... My ears had heard of you but now my eyes have seen you. Therefore I despise myself and repent in dust and ashes" (Job 42;2-6).

Indeed, I despise myself and repent in dust and ashes.

✝

Theresa Ip Froehlich is an ordained minister, professional life coach, writer, and conference speaker. She is a native of Hong Kong, wife to Hervey for twenty-nine years, and mother of two grown children.

THURSDAY

"What Difference Does It Make?"
James Prescott

Rhythm.

We all have one.

Right at the core of our being there is a rhythm to our lives. On a purely physical level, there is a heartbeat. The pace of that heartbeat, the rhythm of it, depends on what we do with the rest of our lives, what rhythm our lives beat to.

Lent is a time when we stop and re-examine that rhythm. It's an opportunity to go back to the core of who we are and what we believe, and reexamine what our life is really about, and where we honestly are with God.

This Lent I have given things up – a common theme during Lent – but I have also taken something up.

Two years ago I took part in a discipleship program, a mission into your own life if you will, which involved carrying on with my regular life – job, church, hobbies etc – but with one subtle yet crucial difference.

Jesus would be first.

For 40 days, I would live intentionally for Jesus, deliberately orientate my life around Him – and part of that included daily prayers and Bible studies, on top of regular serving, tithing and regularly attending group meetings.

It was a very fruitful process, during which I grew closer to God and realized I could do the spiritual disciplines each day if I wanted to. My rhythm changed, life seemed to have purpose, and I was actually disappointed when it finished.

This year, I decided to for Lent to do something similar – to do the Bible studies, daily prayers every morning – which is the worst time of day for me to do that, as I'm definitely not a morning person, so it would require self-discipline.

Not quite the same intensity as two years ago and not such a big commitment, but enough to be different to what I was used to.

So in doing this I took up something new for Lent.

I also gave up things for Lent. Most prominently, chocolate (which of course no one ever does), and take-aways.[12]

Now I've managed to stay off the take-aways so far, but I have given in to the chocolate – and staying off the take-aways is proving tough, though I'm being successful so far.

But in taking up something new, I've done fine so far. The decision to read the Bible each morning and say a set prayer at the start of this day, and have hourly prayer reminders, is working so well. My day is starting much better, I feel more positive about each day and a real sense of peace when I go to work or church or anywhere.

God has been speaking into my heart and giving me a peace.

There is another side to this. It's also allowed God space to get in and really deal with some difficult, painful issues as well. I have found at various points God speaking to me about His grace, about my own failings, and it's been somehow easier to sit down and examine myself and deal with those issues.

Most of them being about control.

You see I like being in control. I think on many levels we all do.

It's one of the things many of us struggle with, giving control of our hearts to God, dying to ourselves and allowing Jesus to raise us up to a new life hidden in Him. I have found that giving into temptation to eat chocolate for example is something that I do to exercise control, because there is a part of me that doesn't want to give up control.

Because giving up something for Lent involves giving up control.

In the end, the difference giving up certain things and beginning new habits make over Lent is that they help us confront our issues of control.

Lent leads up to Easter, which is all about the ultimate giving up of control, the ultimate surrender on the cross – a surrender we are all called to model.

Surrender is at the heart of our faith, giving up control and surrendering it to Jesus who Himself surrendered all for us. And in the process, like what I did when I first did my discipleship course, and in what I have already experienced this year, we How much are you willing to surrender to Jesus this Lent?

✝

James Prescott is a writer, author and blogger from Sutton, near London. He blogs at jamesprescott.co.uk on finding divine hope in a broken world. He is author of the book 5 Steps to Encouragement and the devotional Reflections on Encouragement, which is available for free on his blog. Follow him on Twitter at @JamesPrescott77.

Friday

"It's Time to Go Back to the Desert"
Martha Hopler

It's time to go back to the desert. It's time sit with the God above and realize it's not 40 years… it's forty days. I will go as Jesus did after he was reminded of his call to ministry. I will enter Lent with silence and seriously give up something I have found so helpful in my journey. Not just half way but all the way. This part of the journey is mine. It is not about what everyone else should do: it's about me and God – and I am not alone. This will be the Lent of all Lents for it will lead to new. It will lead to living into who I was created to be:

I am a warrior princess
I am a child of God
I am a woman who loves with all she has and then gives a bit more
And I am ready for the new race… The race of love and truth together.

The 'giving up' is not to say what I had was a bad thing, it is so I can "trade one addiction for another" (Tim Phillips).[13] And 'tis not forever! It's for forty days because I serve a God of Mercy and Grace. I choose this day to give up TV for Forty Days because it will create space for a new day.

I have learned over the last years as I was introduced to Lent that for me this is what it is about. It is about giving up something so I can be in a space that is different. It creates discipline and anyone who knows me knows I hate discipline. I hate the square I have been boxed into… meaning those times that it has been demanded of me to be what works for the group. I have been boxed in a corner where all I have known is anger and screaming at time.

Even as I write these words I hear those who want to take my journey and make it theirs and then they will argue with me about why it will not work. Trust me; I have had all the difficulty in relationship. I love my favorite shows. I love connecting with people. TV it has worked in places where I had nothing in common with another and yet our personalities find common ground and connection through story. I hate it when people make broad sweeping statements about TV as if God is never there… For I have watched amazing shows where whole discussions regarding God are more of a church experience than church itself.

This forty days, for me, is acknowledging just how much I would rather live in the pretend – in the place where God has made all things right. I have been on a journey toward choosing life and the purpose of God for ten years. Not that I have not lived for God for all of my adult life and not to say that after this forty days I will have arrived, but to say that I will be more focused in moving toward what I have believe to be a call. However I must warn you that those who want to believe that know that I am subject to forgetting that this journey continues beyond these 40 days... It really is 40 years and I am still in the middle but closer to end. That is a story for another day. But for now I will choose forty days of no TV and journal about it every day... Forty entries and moving into the New.

Easter is coming.

Martha Hopler a social worker for 15 years in Philadelphia before moving to Seattle where she attended The Seattle School of Theology & Psychology. She is now a social worker, medical case manager at Project Access Northwest. She attends Seattle's First Seattle Baptist Church.

SATURDAY

"Struggling with Lent"
Julie Clawson

So Lent begins again and honestly I have no idea what I'm doing. I've been struggling with the whole thing. I didn't grow up in churches that observed Lent. It was only in college that I was even exposed to the whole concept. I would hear my friends discussing what they wanted to give up for the season – chocolate, TV, soft drinks – as well as hear them complain about how Easter couldn't arrive soon enough. But in truth it all seemed strange. I didn't really understand Lent, but the whole give up something you like was just an odd observance.

I totally understand the idea of being disciplined and of using one's extra time or craving to draw closer to God. That's in theory at least how it's supposed to work. But it all seemed sort of hollow to me. What lasting spiritual effect is there of not eating chocolate, complaining about it, putting others out who happen to serve it, and then resuming consumption come Easter? Or what's the point of giving up TV when you know that you'll just catch up on those episodes of "Lost" on TiVo or DVD after Easter?

What confuses me even more is the tendency to give up relational things for Lent. I've had friends give up using a cell phone – which just made it really annoying for us (or their employer) to reach them. Others give up going out with friends and others give up the whole Facebook, Twitter, blog thing. While I understand how such things can be addictions, it just seems counter-intuitive to the ideals of Lent to separate ourselves from community.

So this is where I'm sure I offend, but its something I've been struggling with. I just don't see the purpose of Lent to be this perfunctory elimination of some random thing we like whose loss we endure simply until Easter. It's just too individualistic – it's all about me, my sacrifice, and (hopefully) my relationship with God. And while I admit to and am grateful for the personal message of the gospel, this perspective seems to forget that part of the message of the gospel (and of Lent) is that of righting relationships. The gospel is not just about us – it's not just about getting our own butts into heaven or making sure we feel close to God. It's also about loving our neighbors, seeking justice for the oppressed, and being part of the body of Christ.

So that's why I am uncomfortable with reducing Lent to chocolate or a few episodes of "American Idol." During Lent we are called to right our relationships with God and with others. So I'm more inclined to instead of giving up Facebook use it more deliberately – trying to be more aware of the simple everyday parts of my friends lives. I don't want to give up food simply for the sake of giving it up – I want to instead show love to others by eating food that was ethically sourced. I want to discipline my life to be more aware, more involved, and more loving. I want the season of Lent to transform me in ways that extend beyond Easter.

That said, I'm at a loss how to proceed this season. I want to love others and build community, but right now I'm still struggling to figure out how. It would be easy to simply eliminate something from my life, but I'm beginning to understand that perhaps it is better to build. But of course, that's a lot messier. So I'm still trying to figure it out.

Julie Clawson is a mother, writer, and former pastor who lives in Austin, TX, with her family. Julie is the author of Everyday Justice: The Global Impact of Our Daily Choices *and* The Hunger Games and the Gospel: Bread, Circuses, and the Kingdom of God. *She can be found at julieclawson.com.*

First Week of Lent:

Journey into the Brokenness of Our Inner Selves

ENTER THE JOURNEY

> "Create in me a clean heart O God and renew a right
> spirit within me" (Ps 51:10).

Read Psalm 51 in unison and then spend time in silence meditating on its implications for your life.

- Get each person to look into a mirror, and using a felt-tip marker or soap, write or draw onto your reflection words and symbols that represent your anxieties and fears. When you are ready, spray glass cleaner onto the mirror and wipe it clean.
- Pray together for God's cleansing in your hearts.

Reflect on those things in your life that focus you on yourself rather than on God. Discuss the following questions:

- What is one thing you struggle with that distracts you from a whole-hearted commitment to Christ? Write down your areas of struggle on a piece of paper.
- How could you use this first week of Lent to initiate a new spiritual discipline that would bring reconciliation and healing in your place of struggle? Some possibilities you might like to consider are:
  - Free up an extra fifteen minutes each day to pray and read the Scripture.
  - Memorize one new Scripture verse each day.
  - Take time each day to read a chapter from a book on spiritual disciplines, such as Richard Foster's *Celebration of Discipline*. In what way could you help each other maintain this discipline?

- Choose a day during this first week of Lent to fast. Use meal times for special prayers. Focus specifically on your failures and broken places, seeking repentance and asking God for forgiveness.
- Seek out one person that you have held a grudge against or treated unjustly and seek forgiveness. Is there an action you need to take to make restitution?

A Litany of Repentance

God, all-loving and all-caring,
We come before you with hesitant steps and uncertain motives.
Our hearts are parched from wandering in a desert of sin.
We want to sweep out the corners where sin has accumulated,
And uncover the places where we have strayed from your truth.
Our hearts are parched from wandering in a desert of sin.
We ask for courage to open our eyes and unstop our ears,
To be aware of all that distracts us from a whole-hearted commitment to Christ.
Our hearts are parched from wandering in a desert of sin.
We want to see ourselves as you do and live our lives as you intended,
Expose the empty and barren places where we have not allowed you to enter.
Our hearts are parched from wandering in a desert of sin.
Reveal to us our half-hearted struggles,
Where we have been indifferent to the pain and suffering of others.
Our hearts are parched from wandering in a desert of sin.
Create in us a clean heart, O God, and put a right Spirit within us,
Nurture the faint stirrings of new life where your spirit has rooted and begun to grow.
Our hearts are parched from wandering in a desert of sin.
We long for your healing light to transform us into the image of Christ,
For you alone can bring new life and make us whole.
In your mercy, shine upon us, O God, and make our path clear before us.

Pause to remind yourself of your own brokenness and need for repentance.

God of mercy, come
Into the hidden places of our hearts.
Christ of compassion, come
Into the broken places of our world.
Spirit of life, come
Into the polluted places of our lives.
Forgive us, heal us, redeem us,
Lead us from death to eternal life.

Read Scripture passages for the day.

Pause to reflect on the gospel and spend time thinking about those things that vie for your attention and distract you from a whole-hearted commitment to Christ.

Write down your areas of struggle on a piece of paper. If you have a wooden cross available, nail or tape your distractions to the cross. Alternatively you may like to place them in a fireplace or a bowl and set them alight. Discuss how you could use this Lenten season to bring reconciliation and healing in these places.

Our Father in heaven, hallowed be your name. Your Kingdom come, your will be done, on earth as in heaven. Give us today our daily bread. Forgive us our sins, as we forgive those who sin against us. Lead us not into temptation, but deliver us from evil. For the kingdom, the power and the glory are yours. Now and forever. Amen.

God, you are good and upright, and you instruct sinners in your ways,
Show us how to break down the barriers separating us from each other.
Lead us through the wilderness sin has created to find new life.
Forgive us for the times we have abandoned the poor, the disabled, and the homeless,
Teach us to live by the law of love in unity, peace, and concord
Lead us through the wilderness sin has created to find new life.
Forgive us for the ways we exclude people of different race, culture, or gender
Guide us that we may come to mutual understanding and care
Lead us through the wilderness sin has created to find new life.
Draw us into your community to embrace those with whom we need to be reconciled,
Grant that all who seek to heal divisions between peoples may have hope.
Lead us through the wilderness sin has created to find new life.
Show us your ways, O Lord,
Teach us your paths and guide us towards your truth.
Lead us through the wilderness sin has created to find new life.

Pause to offer your own prayers of repentance and forgiveness.

Go into the world,
Knowing your life has been touched by the triune God.
You are cleansed by the mercy of God,
You are surrounded by the love of Christ,
You are filled with the power of the Spirit.

Go into the world,
Knowing you are being changed,
You are renewed by the mercy of God,
You are graced with the love of Christ,
You are empowered by the power of the Spirit.
Go into the world and be transformed.
Amen.

Monday

"Walking in Darkness"
Kimberlee Conway Ireton

As Lent approached this year, I found myself in a dark place. This darkness was triggered when I learned I was expectedly pregnant with our third child. It deepened as my pregnancy made me sick. And it became black as night when a dear friend's seemingly healthy daughter was suddenly diagnosed with leukemia.

I do not like living in darkness. I do not like feeling alone and afraid. I do not like wondering where God is. And I especially do not like the agnosticism that creeps into the darkness with me, whispering its words of skepticism and doubt along my skin and in my heart.

But I have learned that I cannot run from the darkness. I can only walk through it. Walking in the way of Jesus, this Lent, for me, is walking by faith rather than sight, by hope rather than conviction.

I want to believe the good news of the incarnation, the crucifixion, the resurrection, and on my best days, I do believe it. But I confess there are days, and lately there have been many of them, when I don't believe this, when I live in fear that it is not true, when I live in fear that God either is not real or else cannot be trusted.

Such fear undermines my very identity, the bedrock of who I usually believe myself to be: a beloved daughter of the God who gives good and perfect gifts. The darkness grows deeper.

But then, words. Words as often as anything else pull me back to the light of faith when I am wandering in the darkness. I was comforted last month to read these words of George MacDonald. He put them in the mouth of one of his characters, an aging pastor who is facing death and wondering if his life has somehow been misspent, if somehow all that he preached and claimed to believe wasn't really true after all. But then he writes,

> Even if there be no hereafter, I would live my time believing in a grand thing that ought to be true, if it is not....Let me hold by the better than the actual and fall into nothingness off the same

precipice with Jesus and John and Paul and a thousand more, who were lovely in their lives, and with their deaths make even the nothingness into which they have passed like the garden of the Lord.[14]

When I read those words, I wept. For they reminded me that I can choose to believe even if I don't feel that belief.

And so on those days when I don't quite believe, I look away from myself, my feelings, my fears. I look out and around, noticing small things that are good: cherry blossoms, a hug from my daughter, a box of new-to-me maternity clothes from a friend. I give thanks for these small mercies, choosing to see them as gifts from God even when I don't believe it. I give thanks that the darkness is not so dark that I cannot make that choice.

On those days when I doubt, I cling all the harder to Jesus, whose way is the way of truth, the truth that sets me free to live and to love in the midst of suffering, the truth that frees me to choose that suffering will render me beautiful rather than bitter and compassionate rather than callous.

On those days when I feel afraid, I cling to His promise that He is with me, that He does not shrink from darkness, that He will never forsake or abandon me.

I choose to trust him.

And eventually, the choosing becomes easier, the darkness lifts, and walking in Jesus' way is not quite such a struggle…for a while. But the darkness will always return, often unexpectedly. That is why I need Lent, because it bears witness to the reality of darkness, of doubt, of fear, of pain. And it carries me through those real places, real experiences into one that is more fully and truly Real: the Reality of Resurrection, of Light, of Life.

For now, it's still Lent. I still walk in darkness. But I am beginning to see glimmers of that Light. I am beginning to walk by sight again, with conviction. I give thanks to God for this mercy, too.

✝

Kimberlee Conway Ireton lives with her husband and four children in Seattle. She is the author of The Circle of Seasons: Meeting God in the Church Year *and* Cracking Up: A Postpartum Faith Crisis. *She may be found at http://kimberleeconwayireton.net.*

Tuesday

"Lent Begins with Listening to Where God is Leading..."
Beth Stedman

My husband and I have been talking a lot about really entering into Lent and about using it as a time to cleanse our bodies, our lives and our hearts. We had been talking about some pretty extreme disciplines we wanted to try and engage in – including going Vegan for Lent. But, as Lent drew closer we started to hear a different message from God...

We started to hear God asking us to be present with where we are – to not try and make things happen – to accept that we can do nothing on our own and in our own strength and to open our hands and hearts to where he wants to lead us and the place in life that he has given us right now.

Over the past little bit I have been thinking a lot about this verse from John 15:"I am the vine; you are the branches. If a man remains in me and I in him, he will bear much fruit; apart from me you can do nothing."[15]

The question, "What does it mean to remain in Christ?" has been circling in my head a lot lately. I can't say that I've figured it out – I haven't. But, I think that one part of it is to rest in trust and allow him to work instead of trying to force things myself. I realize that I do a lot in my own strength and power. I like being in control. I don't like trusting others, and I especially don't like trusting God. But, that's exactly what I feel like He's calling me to right now. He keeps reminding me that apart from him I can do nothing.

In the past few months God has slowly taken away a lot of security from my husband and I. He has slowly lead us to a place in various areas of our lives where we've had to trust him, and wait on him and where we haven't been able to just do things in our own strength or timing. But, there were still things I was holding on to, I still felt like there were things that I could bring and offer and do. But the past few weeks something has happened that I have no control over, that I can't do at all. And it's made that phrase "apart from me you can do nothing" sink in for me in a new way. In this situation I can't make anything happen, I can't control the outcome, but there are small things that I can do to help create a fertile environment for God to work and I think it's given me a picture of how God wants to work with me in other areas of my life. He wants me to stop grasping for the outcomes that I want, stop trying to control things and instead just remain with him, dwell with him and in doing so create a fertile environment for him to move and work and lead me on this journey.

The call of Lent for me this year is a call to let go, to stop striving, to trust and lean back into God's open arms with reckless abandon. It is a call to remain in him and dwell intimately with him. It is a call to let go of my nagging doubt and distrust and to fall fully into Christ. It is a call to stop striving and fully recognize that it is only in Him that I move and breathe and have my being and apart from him I can do nothing.

That is what I feel God is calling me to this Lent. I'm not sure exactly what it will look like, but I want to follow.

Rejoicing in the journey.

✝

Bethany Stedman is a stay-at-home mom with two kids. She loves to write and is currently working on her first novel. She blogs about family, faith and food at www.bethstedman.com.

Wednesday

"Suffering and Hope: A Meditation on Miscarriage and Romans 5:3-5"
Jill Aylard Young

[3] Not only so, but we also glory in our sufferings, because we know that suffering produces perseverance; [4] perseverance, character; and character, hope. [5] And hope does not put us to shame, because God's love has been poured out into our hearts through the Holy Spirit, who has been given to us. (Romans 5:3-5, NIV)

As congregants poured out into the lobby at the close of the church service on Sunday – the Presbyterian church in Pennsylvania where my husband is pastor – I made my way straight over to a young woman who had just found out at 12-weeks that the little life within her was no longer alive. She knew that I too had experienced a similar miscarriage a few months before and so we immediately embraced with knowing and tears. We had rejoiced together in her long awaited pregnancy. Now we were sorrowing together and processing the loss as fellow Christians with a faith and hope that doesn't diminish the reality of pain.

My husband had just preached a sermon on Romans 5:3-5 and this was the backdrop as we shared with each other. The truths in this Scripture felt palpable as we stood together. In the course of our conversation she said both that this experience had been the worst of her life and that she had never experienced such grace and love from the people of God surrounding her. Suffering and hope were mingling.

As I came away from our conversation I realized how fresh my own sorrow from my miscarriage was still, even as I was joyful about my very new and unannounced pregnancy. Just a few hours later my second miscarriage began.

Disbelief, anger, emptiness….a lot of questions, aching disappointment!

We are not protected from suffering as we follow Jesus. We are subject to the same risks in this life.

So how is suffering different as we walk with Jesus? It certainly doesn't mean that we don't struggle, question, resist, and just simply hurt! But suffering provides opportunity for the Holy Spirit's work within us, to grow our character and

45

deepen our hope. I had hoped for a second child (and still do though I'm an older mom who got started later on marriage and family). I already had joyful images in my head of a family of four, of a sibling for our dear daughter Grace, of another grandchild for my dad who a year ago lost his wife, my mother.

As I struggle with this unexpected loss during this Lent, I feel that tug of the Holy Spirit within me to a hope that is deeper than my pictures of how I want my future to be…A hope rooted in the love of God, poured into my heart even in the midst of sorrow, disappointment, unmet longings… a hope in God's love that is not dependent on how the circumstances of life work out. This I have learned through dark times in the past and this I must learn again and again.

By God's mercy may we follow Christ in our suffering, opening our hearts to his love and staying in faith even as we doubt, ache, and resist.

Rev. Jill Young, ordained in the Presbyterian Church (USA) in Sept 2013 after earning her MDiv at Princeton Theological Seminary in 2008, is the Protestant Campus Minister at Bloomsburg University. Originally from the Los Angeles area and then Seattle area, she now lives in Elysburg, Pennsylvania with her husband Rev. Matthew Young (pastor at Elysburg Presbyterian Church) and their daughter Grace. They are expecting a 2nd child due Christmas Eve! Jill served on the board of MSA for several years.

THURSDAY

"Lent with Children"
Kristin Carroccino

Every few years during Lent, the Revised Common Lectionary offers my favorite reading from the Bible, the message Jesus speaks in the synagogue after having spent time fasting in the desert and being tempted by Satan. He is clear-eyed, wiry, ready, and takes the words of his forbear Isaiah and proclaims his new ministry:

> The spirit of the Lord GOD is upon me, because the LORD has anointed me; he has sent me to bring good news to the oppressed, to bind up the brokenhearted, to proclaim liberty to the captives, and release to the prisoners; to proclaim the year of the Lord's favor, and the day of vengeance of our God; to comfort all who mourn. (Isaiah 61:1-2, NRSV)

This passage is always so appropriate for me by the time I reach Lent, a season we are called upon to be turning our gaze inward to search out and reveal those broken places within and then outward to see that brokenness mirrored in the world around us. By this season I have moved through the glorious celebration of the birth of Jesus at Christmas, and considered new epiphanies for myself during the weeks that follow. Lent arrives, and as we walk with Jesus through the days of his earthly ministry – represented by forty days in late winter and early spring, I find myself more mindful of the ways I would like my life to reflect my Teacher's. I also find myself on an annual basis, wondering how to convey the richness of this season to my children, without it seeming frightening and focused on death.

Lent has the ability to strip us bare and often, as parents of young children, we often feel we have nothing left to give up, we are spent – we recognize poverty of spirit and brokenness at every bend in the road when we wake to face the mirror and wails of complaint anew every morning. Lent, then, can also be a season of finding faith in ourselves again. Some of us who have practiced Lent for many years must turn to giving up being unkind to ourselves and take on gentle practices of renewal. Much as the thick mud of late winter covers a wild array of daffodils and trillium, so, too, must we trust that beauty and renewal lay waiting to grow beneath the often thick morass of our dailiness.

So, I begin with focusing on Jesus' promise to bind up my broken heart, and I consider that he says the greatest commandment is to love myself, God and then others in the same way. This doesn't reduce or blind my effort to see creation and humanity suffering, but reminds me that I must be on a healing path to better live out my calling to lend others a hand when called upon. I think about the stories that are happening in Jesus' life during these weeks when he is living out his calling – being gentle with people, healing, praying by himself, crying out for justice. And then, we talk about those stories as a family and seek to turn the tradition of Lent from being a time of asceticism and extreme penance into a time where our children may start to embrace some of the stories of Jesus for themselves.

We put a mug in the center of the table and add at least forty slips of paper bearing names of individual friends and family members and pray for one name each day during our meals. We make a practice of "spring cleaning" and "making room for Jesus" by cleaning out our cupboards and dusting our light fixtures to "allow more light into our lives." We look in the garden, and find bulbs that have "died" in winter mud now pushing up, showing exuberant color. We find caterpillars and imagine their "death" and "resurrection" as butterflies. Maybe we will do a service project each week based on one of the stories of Jesus' ministry – take a meal to someone in need, learn more about our community and the captives and broken hearts who may be living just down the street. We look for the signs of the good news that Jesus came to bring – stories of hope and not just oppression. We talk about trusting the goodness in the world that God has made. We are kind to ourselves. We pay attention. We wait. And then we approach Holy Week with quietness but with also a suppressed joy about what will happen at the end of the week. We trust that Easter always comes again, even when things and people around us speak of death.

In her fabulous and classic book about celebrating the liturgical seasons, *To Dance with God*, author Gertrud Mueller Nelson writes this in her introduction to the season of Lent:

> Thinking about Lent is not my favorite thing to do. In fact, I rather hate it. Every year, when the subject comes up, I see myself resist. I can think about Advent, about expectancy. It holds some concerns, but to be impregnated with new life is a rather hopeful subject. During Advent we rejoice as we open ourselves to the mysteries of the marriage of heaven to earth. But in Lent we come to know that the only way to our own healing and wholeness comes paradoxically through dismembering—an appallingly painful process which life offers us, ready or not, and which Lent gives us the form and meaning for. 'They have pierced my hands and feet, they have numbered all my bones.' We engage dismemberment and

atonement so that we may be transformed through the Easter mysteries and arrive at 'at-one-ment.'[16]

As we move into this season of dismembering, of moving from life to death to life again, let us hold on with open hearts and hands, knowing that this great story and these practices are meant for our good, to draw us ever closer into love and healing. That Jesus is right there, waiting to free us and bind up broken hearts.

Kristin Carroccino is a writer and photographer and volunteer for Mustard Seed Associates. She lives in Seattle with her husband Michael and two young children. More of her writing can be found at boatswithoutoars.blogspot.com, which is a record of a cross country journey studying Episcopal churches in the summer of 2012.

FRIDAY

"Depression and the Living God"
Anonymous Contributor

I don't hunger and thirst for much. I just hunger and thirst to escape depression. There, I've said it. But I'm not able to add my name to this statement. I need to be anonymous.

I am a middle-aged pastor of a suburban congregation of around 150-160. Every week I stand and declare that Jesus forgives our sins and restores us to life. Yet I am bound by pain which reaches back into my infant past, pain that I have only just become aware of through therapy, pain that I have not yet faced—and fear to face even now.

I have grown up being driven to 'repair' the world, to 'make a difference', trying to make it better so that others don't suffer the way I do. I fear I have mixed that up with what it means to be a Christian, and to be a pastor. When I fail, there is a kind of voice within my therapist calls the 'savage god' who accuses me of being —wait for it—less than perfect. I have confused that voice with the Living God. Sometimes the only thing that protects me from suicidal thoughts is a sense of compassion I can find within myself for those with whom I could be rightfully angry with. I would dearly like to find 'rest for my soul'.

I see a therapist several times a week. I take antidepressants at the maximum dose. I pray. I believe. I love my congregation, and I have the good fortune to pastor a supportive, wonderful community. The people know I suffer with depression, because I've spoken about it from the pulpit. It seemed important for me to do so to help fellow-sufferers who felt shame for their illness. Yet only a few know how much I suffer; I want to protect the congregation. I want them to know the freedom that is theirs in Christ. In fact, when I lead worship I do feel like the burden is lifted for a while. I find that I can step outside the constrictions of the pain I feel and be with the people. I don't mean that I'm overly demonstrative, just that I know that inner freedom for a time and my smile is genuine.

I don't think I'm living a lie. My problem isn't authenticity; it's just pain that has dogged me since the nursery.

I'm sure there will be others posting in this series who want justice and peace for all. So do I, and so does my community. I want the kingdom of God to come. I know it is here now, in the midst of my pain, our pain. I know that in Bonhoeffer's great words, 'only a suffering God can help' and I take comfort in that. I know Christ's strength is in my weakness. I just want to feel it all the way through.

This Lent, I expect to put one foot in front of the other and walk towards Holy Week and the Triduum. I rejoice at the destination of the Empty Tomb. But I fear there's still quite a bit of me mouldering in that tomb, and I hunger and thirst for it to live.

✝

This author is a fellow pilgrim on the journey with Jesus.

Saturday

"Thin Spaces"
Paula Mitchell

Heaven touches earth
the veil separating God and us
shimmers and for a moment in time-
we find ourselves
standing in God's presence
holy ground-
Where like Moses we stop, look,
take off our shoes.
God breaks through our hard packed soil,
shattering our well-defended walls
touches our heart with his love and grace
thin space, holy ground.
Jesus, love of God embodied
for thirty-three years
God's light shining
in the darkness
Chaos—
of our world bringing
Life, Light, Love
Freely giving tender mercy, loving kindness, forgiveness, grace
God who so loves the world
so loves us-
he gave us his only begotten son
whosoever believes in him will not perish
in the deep darkness
but be given life eternal.
The Saints, too, each a thin space unique in their own way
holy ground, fertile soil, pounded thin
by circumstance, pain, suffering
compassion birthed in the soft soil of holy lives given to God.
They prayed that the life of Christ might take root, grow, and produce fruit-
holy ground, fertile ground, given to God

heaven touching earth—thin space
fully alive for the glory of God
Creation, too, a sacrament of God's presence
where heaven breaks earth open
glimmers of God's beauty
mountains, oceans, sky,
magnificent, radiant, translucent
reflecting heaven
thin spaces
holy ground
if only we have eyes to see.
Mary, too, a thin space
Where the life of Christ took root and grew.
She, too, holy ground, humble soil, a thin space
Bearing Christ in the rich soil of
humiliation and suffering
yet with great joy and gladness
for unto to us a child is born,
a son given, you shall call his name Jesus.
Not an easy path, full of suffering,
her heart broken by the darkness.
But God promises that the darkness can never, ever extinguish the light
Her yes makes me want to take off my shoes
her life a thin space
holy ground
radiant with his light.
Paul learned
he is made perfect not in his strength
but in his weakness.
Thin enough to be broken
Thin enough for the life of Jesus
to break through
reminding us all
it is no longer we who live but the life we now live is Christ's own life
mysterious, embodied, thin space
Christ in me the hope of glory
not my glory
His-
What about you?
Do you hunger and thirst for thin spaces?
People who let the light of Christ radiate in them
Light bearers

Christ bearers
Those who carry the death of Christ in their bodies
so they may carry the life of Christ into the world.
Into your world
that you might know his presence in and with you.
Those who bear his wounds, who share his heart,
who bring compassion and peace
To the chaos of our times
To the chaos of our lives
Thin spaces
Holy ground
Sometimes I wonder,
Can I be a thin space?
It's what I want-
what I hunger and thirst for-
what I'm afraid of-
To become so thin
Radiant
That the life of Christ
shines through me
radiates from me, is embodied in me
whether I know it or not.
So I no longer live but the life I live in my body is the life
of Christ living in me
Thin space
Holy ground
For the light shines in the darkness
And the darkness can never ever put it out...

Paula Mitchell is a Spiritual Director, retreat facilitator, writer, wife, and mother of four grown sons. She is the founder and program director of Doorways Ministries, providing days of prayer, Ignatian retreats, and a 9 month program based on the Spiritual Exercises of St. Ignatius as ways of deepening our lives with Christ. She is also the coordinator for the Ignatian Spirituality Project, a Jesuit organization dedicated to offering spiritual retreats inspired by Ignatian Spirituality to people experiencing homelessness. Paula brings to Doorways her own desire for deeper intimacy with Jesus, a love of prayer, and a heart to share with others the freedom and joy found in following Jesus.

SECOND WEEK OF LENT:

JOURNEY INTO THE BROKENNESS OF HUNGER

ENTER THE JOURNEY

> "Is not this the kind of fasting I have chosen: ... to share your food with the hungry and to provide the poor wanderer with shelter" (Isaiah 58:6-7).

Begin your weekly meeting by discussing your discipline for the past week. In what ways have you been tempted to take short cuts over the week to avoid or minimize your new discipline? Write your distractions and struggles on a piece of paper. If you have a wooden cross available, nail or tape your distractions to the cross. Alternatively you may like to place them in a fireplace or a bowl and set them alight to symbolize your new freedom from those distractions.

Now focus on the next stage of your journey. Familiarize yourself with some of the facts about poverty. Visit the World Food Programme website at www.wfp.org/hunger. Read through the facts on hunger. How does this make you feel? What can you do to make a difference?

During this second week of Lent, we want to identify with those in our world who are chronically hungry and investigate ways that we can assist them in their struggle to establish food security.

The Mutunga Partnership,[17] based in Melbourne, Australia, and the Two Dollar Challenge[18] in the US are organizations trying to turn the tragic statistics of world hunger into a tool for raising awareness, building a sense of community with the poor, and raising funds for micro-credit development. Both the Mutunga $2 Challenge and the Two Dollar Challenge encourage households to live on a food budget of $2 per person per day for a week and then donate the money they save. This idea doesn't require finding extra cash—just a temporary change in lifestyle. It's a challenge!

We challenge you to take the issue of world hunger seriously. Restrict your food budget to less than $2 per person per day for this second week of Lent. Send the money you save to the Mutunga Partnership or Two Dollar Challenge. Send us your reflections and comments. Appendix I, at the end of this booklet, provides a suggested meal plan and menus for the week.

Discuss these questions with your group:

- What permanent changes would you consider making in your eating habits as a result of this challenge?
- How much money would this save on a monthly basis and how could you use it to make an ongoing difference for those that live in poverty?

For some, restricting your food budget to $2 a day may be too much of a challenge. Here are some other suggestions for the week:

- Each time you shop during the week, buy an extra bag of groceries and donate them to a local food bank.
- Prepare all your meals at home and donate what you would normally spend on eating out to an organization that works with the hungry.
- Halve your food budget for the week and donate the money you save to an organization that works with the hungry.

A LITANY FOR ALL WHO HUNGER

Blessed are you, God of the universe,
Lover of justice and righteousness,
Bringer of freedom and wholeness,
We bow down before you, for your name is holy.
You care for the widow and the orphan,
You grieve for the sick and the dying,
Your compassion is stirred by the poor and the starving,
We bow down before you, for your name is holy.
You are a forgiving God to us.
Though you punish our misdeeds,
You will have mercy on us when we repent,
We bow down before you, for your name is holy.

Pause to remind yourself of the millions around the world who live in poverty.

God, be with us.
Before us to guide us.
Behind us to protect us.
Beside us to befriend us.
Make us aware of your world.
God, be with us.
Give us eyes that see the poor.
Give us ears that hear their cries.
Give us hearts that respond to their needs.
Make us aware of your world.

Read Scripture passages for the day from the Daily Lectionary.

*Pause to remind yourself of times that you have been indifferent to the cries of the poor.
What action can you take to change this?*

**Have mercy on us, son of the living God,
Draw us closer into intimacy with you,
Draw us deeper into a life at one with yours,
Draw us forward into the ways of God's kingdom.**

Our Father in heaven, hallowed be your name. Your Kingdom come, your will be done, on earth as in heaven. Give us today our daily bread. Forgive us our sins, as we forgive those who sin against us. Lead us not into temptation, but deliver us from evil. For the kingdom, the power and the glory are yours. Now and forever. Amen.

God, you have set us free,
Not free to do what we please,
But free to love you with our whole hearts gladly.
Free to love our neighbors as we do ourselves.
God, we need to know your freedom.
Free us from our selfishness,
Free us from our indifference to those in need,
Free us to love and serve you with all our being.
God, we want to live in your freedom.
Free us to show compassion to all who are cast aside,
Free us to share generously so that none will lack provision,
Free us to live in love and mutual care.
God, you call us to freedom,
Freedom to love you with our hearts and souls and minds,
Freedom to love our neighbors as ourselves,
Freedom to live in your kingdom ways.
God, may we enter the freedom of your kingdom today.

Pause to offer up your own prayers for those who face hunger around the world.

Let God's compassion bloom in us,
And God's righteousness bear fruit.
Let God's generosity be harvested.
And God's life be born afresh in us.
Let God's light shine in hidden places,
And God's love take root and grow.
Amen.

Monday

"Giving Things Up Does Not Imply Loss"
Christine Sine

"The cost of progress is not whether we add more to the abundance of those who have much; it is whether we provide enough for those who have too little."[19]

Three billion people—almost half the world population—live on less than $2.50 per day. According to UNICEF, 22,000 children die each day due to poverty. And they "die quietly in some of the poorest villages on earth, far removed from the scrutiny and the conscience of the world. Being meek and weak in life makes these dying multitudes even more invisible in death." [20]

Hunger is not just a problem in poor countries, however. In the United States the number of households living on $2 a day or less, per person, surged by 130% between 1996 and 2011, according to the National Poverty Center.[21] Thirty eight million people are at risk of hunger, and, the US has the highest infant mortality rate of any Western nation.[22] Forecasts show the price of corn rising by another 25 percent by 2020 due to the increased demand for ethanol, the production of which took 30% of the US cereal crop in 2008. Filling an SUV's tank with ethanol can use enough corn to feed a person for a year.[23]

The reality of hunger in our world is horrifying and statistics like these are both daunting and overwhelming. Even more daunting can be the implications for my own life and priorities. What am I willing to give up to help those less fortunate than myself? I could not help but think of that as I read these words from Joan Chittister's book *The Liturgical Year.* "Giving things up does not imply loss. In fact because of what we give up, we stand to gain a great deal."[24] We often think that giving things up means sacrifice, loss and decreased satisfaction in life, but is that really true?

For one week each year we commit ourselves to the $2 challenge for the week – restricting our budget in order to free up money to give to those in poverty. It is a week of giving up. It means the loss of meals eaten out and the cutting out of some of my favourite but expensive foods – like avocados in salads and papaya for breakfast (yes I know they don't grow in Seattle but they are a couple of my non-local indulgences). Another quote from Joan Chittister is helpful here: "Self-indulgence, the preening of self for the sake of self, blocks out the cries of the rest of the world, making us deaf to anything beyond ourselves."[25]

Restricting my diet in this way has made me more aware of the cries of the poor and of their daily struggle to survive. I can choose to live on $2/day, and if I indulge and go over my budget it doesn't really matter. The poor have no other option.

What I am realizing is that it does matter for me too. I have high cholesterol, partly genetic but there are other factors that contribute as well. Most of my friends are stunned because they think that Tom and I eat more healthily than most, but I have allowed my weight to creep up in the last couple of years, so I need to lose twenty pounds in the next few months. And that means giving up excuses like "It's not fun to walk in the rain" for not getting out to exercise. It also means giving up the occasional indulgence in fish and chips – unless the fish is grilled or broiled. Even in the midst of these simple losses, I stand to gain a great deal. Eating more healthily means gaining better health, not just now but hopefully in the future too.

What am I willing to give up for my faith I wonder in order to gain the "heart healthy" rewards it could hold for the future? What am I willing to give up of my own prosperity so that others at the margins can survive? These are questions I continue to grapple with. We live such comfortable lives. It is easy to make excuses for self indulgence rationalizing it with thoughts of "God wants to bless me."

Now I am not denying that God wants to bless us, all I question is the assumption that blessing comes in the form of self-centeredness and self-satisfaction. Self-centeredness makes the self the centre of the universe. Again in the words of Joan Chittister: "The notion that all things were made for our comfort and our control robs those around us of their own gifts. It absorbs the gifts of others; it smothers them under our own; it blinds us to both their needs and their gifts."[26]

The greatest satisfaction of my life has come from enabling others to become more of whom God intends them to be – first through providing healthcare to the poor and the marginalized as I worked on the Mercy Ship and in refugee camps in Thailand and Africa, then through writing, advocacy and mentoring. So what are the ongoing losses God might be asking all of us to partake of so that others can find their freedom and their giftedness?

✛

Christine Sine is the Executive Director of Mustard Seed Associates. She trained as a physician in Australia and developed the medical ministry for Mercy Ships. She now speaks on issues relating to changing our timestyles and lifestyles to develop a more spiritual rhythm for life. She has authored several books including Return to Our Senses: Reimagining How We Pray; Godspace: Time for Peace in the Rhythms of Life; *and* Tales of a Seasick Doctor. *Christine blogs at* http:// godspace-msa.com.

TUESDAY

"Reflections on the Mutunga Challenge"
Grace Caudillo

Feb 21-28, 2007. This week I am trying out the $2 a day food challenge. I made my shopping list, which includes ingredients for a soup, some cheese, beans, rice, and burritos. Bananas and carrots were my fruits and veggies. But as I sat down in front of my very small burrito I couldn't help but look for salsa in the fridge, the one that's been kept there since the beginning of time. I'm not cheating, really, I'm allowing more room in the fridge...

I spaced out my food supply, making sure I had enough to last me till the end of the week. Unfortunately, my stomach was not very happy with this new diet, and I usually only made it to mid-afternoon before I got the shakes, couldn't focus on my work, and my energy sank to below sub-level. The logical solution: indulge in a cup of coffee. By the time dinner rolled around, I was convulsing and had nothing but broth and veggies to calm me down. I begin to wonder if some ice cream that had also been in the freezer since the beginning of time would cure my problem. Again, allowing for more room in the freezer. When I hit the hay, I was weak and not able to think straight, but I dreaded getting up in the morning to face the one fried egg and half a banana that would fill me up for the morning.

In the land of plenty, I should not be going to bed hungry. That was the logical conclusion my mind jumped to. I should indulge along with the richest of the rich. My frustration increased throughout the week because I realized how much I do indulge. In fact, I indulge all the time. My lifestyle is one of the most comfortable and indulging lifestyles there are compared to these people who have nothing, and not even the possibility of anything. I was also frustrated because I am so dependent on my indulgences. I do not know how to live without them, how to maneuver my way around them, how to live with less in a society that screams, "You NEED this!"

The end of the week rolled around, and I unfortunately did not have the successful results of some. In fact, mine were quite opposite. In this defeat, I went back to the source of the challenge: to identify with the poor. I am quite incapable of living like the poor, but I am capable of living in simplicity. I learned that I can look beyond my immediate need and find Christ loving me because I am so poor in spirit. Maybe that week helped prepare me for something greater.

✛

Grace spent her growing-up years in France and now lives in Seattle, Washington. A couple years ago, she tried out the Mutunga $2 Challenge.

Wednesday

"Hungering and Thirsting for God?"
Steve Wickham

In a world of multiplicity, including bounteous sources for satisfaction, we can easily miss the truth that appears right in front of us every moment of every day. The Lord, our living God, is providing us ample food and water in the focused meal of abundance:

> "You're blessed when you've worked up a good appetite for God.
> He's food and drink in the best meal you'll ever eat." ~Matthew 5:6
> (The Message)

But we readily present ourselves before the sizeable and bloating banquets on offer elsewhere and everywhere. The meal of salvation is, contrarily, scant-from-view, in that it requires a search. What is characteristic of humanity is we fall into the arms of convenience, or give up on that search too easily.

If we hunger and thirst for God—for righteousness in true humility—we will win a meal so handsome, it reveals all other meals as junk food. But, then, many people are more than satisfied with food that cannot, in their moment, or in the end, satisfy. No wonder there is so much obesity—the chubbiness of material excess, and where our spirituality shrinks.

When we come before the table of food that materially-stoked others can know nothing about (John 4:32), and we have spiritual enlightenment enough to understand the context and power of such food, we truly have the keys to our world—beyond worldliness. The world was meant to come with God, not function without Divine Presence and Provision.

Indeed, the world without God is a darkly unimaginative reality, promising much, but delivering little. There is a veneer about it, that which, when scratched away, reveals a tribal nastiness that hardly bears recognition in the face of an uninquisitive mind.

The reason many people don't see this veneer covering almost everything is it so implicit in our world, and we see it whenever the world tries to exist there before us without God. The world is a cart; it needs a horse (the Lord) to pull it—to make it functional and, more, meaningful.

And the relevance of the Source of the real food begins to unfold when we find, with everything at our disposal, our meaning has disappeared, or perhaps has never appeared or even existed. Meaning comes first—it has to. What good is there scheduling 'the what' before 'the why'? Why marry for the sake of marrying? Or, why settle for a career in order to earn income when a career is not fulfilling? 'The why' must come first.

We should have noticed, already, that this Divine Meal we speak of comes implicit with the need to get our priorities for time right. We are fed, spiritually, by the fundamental nuances; the spending of our time.

Why did see Israelites chase after water and food in the desert? They were thirsty and hungry—dying from lack of these. Yet, they lacked more the spiritual sustenance and faith of vision. Such faith would have seen them nourished both physically and spiritually. But they chose to negate the spiritual by putting the physical ahead.

We are all Israelites chasing after water and food in our respective deserts. We can have the easy-to-gain water and food; God will give us these and, yet, we won't be blessed. We must thirst and hunger after what is truly significant: the truth and fullness of God. Then we will be filled.

What do we hunger and thirst for: bread or the righteousness of God; water or justice?

✝

Steve Wickham, Pastor of Discipleship and Training at Lakeside Baptist Church, Perth, Western Australia, is a Registered Safety Practitioner and holds degrees in Science, Divinity, and Counseling. Steve writes at: http://epitemnein-epitomic.blogspot.com.au/ and http://tribework.blogspot.com.au/ and http://inspiringbetterlife.blogspot.com.au/.

THURSDAY

"Lent & Women (Multitasking, as so many women do so well)"
Aj Schwanz

The Lenten Reflection guide calls us to reflect on hunger this week: Journey into the Brokenness of Hunger. The author gives global statistics on how many people go hungry, how many people will go hungry, what a typical amount of money for a given meal looks like, and what the picture of present consumption vs. future population figures looks like (*bleak*). It's enough to make me want to put my head under a pillow, or listen to the new U2 album really loud so that I can't hear the worries – then again, listening to our current day St. Bono probably isn't the best "numb out" material. Stinkin' sensitivity to the Spirit.

The guide offers a practice of planning meals using $2.00 per person a day – the worldwide average amount of money available for sustaining life (but actually, many exist on less). Immediately, my defenses went up:

1. But I can't plan around that! I already have things planned out for the week.
2. I don't know how much this stuff cost, and I already have it on hand.
3. I can't provide the boys with nutritious food for that much money.
4. What about my blood sugar issues? I need protein: that's expensive.
5. This takes too much time. I have other things that need to get done.
6. Excuse. Excuse. Excuse. Excuse.

Which brings me to International Women's Day, which is March 8 of each year. Feeding the family tends to fall down the chute as "women's work". How many women don't have the choice of opting out of this practice? How many women make it work – graciously – without their families knowing the work, the labor, the cost behind it – as an act of love – lean into the Lord, meal by meal, to make ends meet?

I've been reading a chronological mash up of Kings and Chronicles lately: talk about a crazy time period. Prosperity, famine, prosperity, famine. Good kings, bad kings, mediocre kings, and everything in between. While the stories of the different rulers run together (Was it Israel or Judah? Tore down high places? Offered pagan sacrifices? Built up defenses? Got hit with disease?), the stories of two women stand out: the woman who fed Elijah and her containers overflowed with flour and oil, and the woman who housed Elisha and he promised she would have a son. One was poor; one was rich. One was asked for hospitality; one offered it. Initially one had a son; one was without. But they both eventually had children, and they both almost lost what they treasured. These women had faith enough to seek out an intercessor: they wrestled with God over the things that were precious to them – the future that they believed God had promised them.

This doesn't happen in every situation. I've seen women pray and plead and fast and ask over and over and over of the Lord to heal their children/husband/ sister/friend: the ill one doesn't make it. It's the faith, the persistence, I see so many women equipped with. Their life circumstances, their struggles, their belief in the future that God has promised them: they keep that in their day-to-day view, driving and drawing them closer to God. Not only do they make do: they flourish. And they reach out to work with intercessors if that's what the situation calls for, pride be damned.

Today I think about the women who've been in my life: my first grade teacher who I deemed would still love me even if my mom was mad at me, a woman who taught my eldest in Sunday School the same songs she taught me at day camp, my mama and her friends and how we kids never had to worry that there were economic hard times – and there were which I'm just finding out about now. Friends, teachers, advisors, writers, singers, knitters, chefs, missionaries, moms, students, pray-ers, intercessors leaning into the leanness of the time and allowing it to transform them more into the image of Christ for the sake of others.

> "The LORD your God in your midst, The Mighty One, will save;
> He will rejoice over you with gladness, He will quiet you with His
> love, He will rejoice over you with singing."[27]

(And we wonder where women get it).

✝

Aj grew up in Northwest U.S., but her roots are of a much more Southern-ly nature. She is a wife, a mama, a daughter and sister. She often chases her son, dog, cat, and the idea of a cat nap. Reading cookbooks, writing, exploring spiritual formation, and sudoku-ing all float her boat. She wonders what it means "to be in process of being transformed into the image of Christ for the sake of others" as a woman: Quaker: young adult: right here and now. She blogs at Quakin' in the 'burbs http:// www.ajschwanz.com/

FRIDAY

"A Lifestyle of Enough"
Eugene Cho

About two years ago, Minhee and I made one of the hardest decisions we've made thus far in our marriage and in our calling as parents.

In our hope to honor a conviction of the Holy Spirit to give up a year's salary, we had begun the two year process of saving, selling, and simplifying in 2007. Our goal was to come up with our then year's wages of $68,000 – in order to launch a movement called One Day's Wages. With only a few months left to come up with the total sum, we were a bit short and decided to sublet our home for couple months and asked some friends if we could stay with them on their couches or their guest room.

Needless to say, it was a very humbling time.

Our instruction for ourselves and our children were very simple:
Each person gets one carry-on bag for their belongings.

I still remember crying the night I told our kids of our plans. This wasn't what I had signed up for; This was by far more difficult that I had imagined; I felt I had failed my wife and children; A deadbeat.

Had I known, there is no way in Hades I would have agreed to this conviction.

But as I look back now, I'm incredibly grateful for this experience. We simplified our lives; Sold off belongings we didn't need. For about 2 years, we agreed as a family not to buy anything beyond our necessities. When we stayed with friends, we were reminded what was most essential in our lives:

It was the people right in front of us.
Faith and Hope in Christ.
My marriage. My children. My community.

In our 2500+ square feet home, it's so easy to get lost in our stuff, our possessions, our rooms, our floors, our gadgets, our TV sets, our personal music listening devices, etc.

We can get so lost in our stuff that we forget – or take for granted – the most important things: relationships.

Two years later, I worry that the invaluable lessons we learned during our season of simplicity may be getting lost on us – again. As most of my readers know, I was recently on sabbatical. It's something I treasure every three years and during my sabbatical, we usually leave Seattle and during our time away, we try to sublet our home – if we can find renters we trust. While it's not something we particularly want to do, it's an important source of income that allows us to travel without financial worries. But in order to sublet the home, we have to minimize and clean up the home…

And so before we left for our 7000+ mile sabbatical road trip, we couldn't believe how much stuff we've accumulated since we gave up our fast of "not buying anything beyond essentials." We couldn't believe the stuff we've accumulated in our closets, our garage, our toy boxes, our offices, etc. And to be honest, the stuff we've accumulated in…our hearts.

And this is from a family that takes great "pride" in simple living!

Again, I'm reminded of the great power in the story of Jesus. There are so many things that compel me about Jesus but one of them is what I call the story of "downward mobility."

It completely contradicts the movement of upward mobility that is pervasive in our culture. We want to upgrade everything at every opportunity:

We want the bestest, the fastest, the   strongest, the mightiest, the largest, the mostest, the most horse powerful-est, the beautiful-est, the most blazing CPU processer-est, and the list goes on and on…

Even as I'm typing this on my lethargically slow netbook, I want…I need…I lust…for the new Mac Air.

But I digress.

Upward mobility never stops. Because we go through this cycle constantly. And the powers to be know this.

Jesus?
The incarnation is the story of how Jesus humbled himself and chose not to exercise his divine rights and, instead, took on flesh and bone and to simultaneously assume full humanity– being fully God but also fully man. Born in a manger to simple commoners, he assumed a simple lifestyle as a carpenter and throughout his life, he owned nothing except the stuff he traveled with.

It's the story of downward mobility.

This is a lesson and a story we have to all get behind. This is the Jesus we have to get behind – not the Jesus of bling bling, the Jesus of total prosperity theology; a Jesus of exclusivity and elitism; a Jesus of total health and prosperity, or the Jesus of "send $49 and we'll mail you this special anointed cloth."

It's not to suggest that we have to adopt a lifestyle of poverty but rather…

A lifestyle of enough.
We have enough. We are blessed and blessed immensely. God has given us enough. God is our enough.

I'm reminded of the wise words of G. K. Chesterton:
"There are two ways to get enough: one is to continue to accumulate more & more. The other is to desire less."

So true. So true.

Perhaps, an easy and one (more) step we can take to grow in "our lifestyle of enough" is to simply give away our birthdays[28] or to consider how we can creatively celebrate the Christmas season in parallel to Jesus' model of downward mobility.

✝

Eugene is the founder and Lead Pastor of Quest Church - an urban, multicultural, and multi-generational congregation in Seattle, Washington. He is also the founder and Executive Director of Q Cafe - an innovative non-profit community cafe & music venue. Eugene and his wife, Minhee, are also the founders of One Day's Wages - "a new movement of people, stories, and actions to alleviate extreme global poverty." Eugene and Minhee have been married for over 15 years, have three children and live in Seattle, Washington.

SATURDAY

"Reading the Bible from the Margins"
Ellen Haroutunian

I once had a conversation with a fellow Christian about what Jesus might be asking us to do about the poor. She insisted that she scrimped and saved and made good decisions all her life in order to have what she has now and those who are poor could do the same. Any discussions about laws or systems that discriminate against the poor (and thus help keep them in the cycle) were moot to her. She sincerely felt that this was the teaching of the scriptures. I recently wrote a blog post about another friend who ministers in the legal system with young women in detention. Those woman are invariably low income folks, and of course, they have made really bad choices in their lives. But this friend understands that the ways in which the poor have been taught to think and understand life and finances are very different from those of us with more privileged lives, and that they need much intervention and mentoring before the things that seem like common sense to us can be understood, much less embraced. She has learned to see through their eyes.

It comes down to seeing. My first friend was unable and angrily unwilling to see through the eyes of those who had had different lives and opportunities than she. I can understand her frustration. It would be easier to "help" the poor if they were like us, that is, if it didn't require that we enter into their worlds to see as they do. It is common for us to assume that others see and experience the world in the same way we do. We also assume that others experience God the same way and read the Bible the same way as well. Miguel A. De La Torre, author of *Reading The Bible From The Margins* says that it's all too easy to assume that the Bible text has one clear meaning that existed in the mind of God and was revealed to the original hearer and we may ascertain what that was and apply it for all time and all people. However, interpretations of the "one meaning" often reflect the dominant culture – an androcentric, white, middle to upper middle class westernized reading. Then, if these interpretations are questioned, we become unsettled and even defensive as if we are messing with the biblical text itself. But just like my first friend, we can remain blind if this one perspective is the only set of interpreting eyes that we have upon the text.

Justo Gonzalez (quoted by Miguel A. De La Torre) shares a story of a sermon preached through the eyes of the marginalized. The community was studying the part of the fourth commandment that says, "six days you shall labor." The pastor asked the congregation how many had worked six days that week, then five, then four, etc. Very few hands went up. Then he asked how many would like to work for six days but were unable to find employment. All of the hands went up. The minister responded, "How then, are we to obey the law of God which commands that we shall work six days, when we cannot find work even for a single day?" Honestly, I had always just skimmed over that part of the commandment. I didn't see.

De La Torre points out that the "eyes" of class privilege blind us to that first part of the commandment. We assume the privilege of being employed. We are oblivious then to the reality of those segments of our society that lack opportunity for gainful employment because of external prejudices towards race, ethnicity or class, or internal things such as brain-addling traumatic stress due to chronic poverty, neglect and abuse. Without being willing to hear and see the text through the eyes of the marginalized we miss this and probably much more. Our blindness keeps us from loving our neighbors as ourselves.

A few years ago I was invited to teach to a group of Christian pastors and leaders in Mozambique. I remember speaking about Sabbath and what it meant to keep that commandment. There with the poor was the struggle of finding the six days of work. I wondered what it would be like to move into discussion of the Sabbath Day, when their six days had not brought them the fruits of labor. However, the Africans seem to grasp a better sense of the need for Sabbath and the Shalom, human flourishing, wellbeing, connectedness, enjoyment and rest that the day was meant to bring, because their culture is much more communally oriented and not as production and success driven as ours. Even so, it became evident to me that they took everything I said as absolute truth and it was hard for them to believe that I truly desired their discussion and input. I became painfully aware that here I was, a white person of privilege standing "over" black Africans in authority as a teacher, just as plenty of white, western, well-meaning missionaries had done so many times before.

What would it be like to see the text through their eyes? It was one of the "help me God" moments. I sensed God say (no honest, I did), "Speak to them about their story." So, with some trepidation, I did so. Mozambique was formerly Portuguese East Africa and at least a million people from that region had been kidnapped and sold into slavery a century and a half before. The Portuguese colonists had since ruled their land and made them into second class citizens. That rule did not end until the latter part of the 20th century. As we reflected on their story aloud, their eyes dropped to their laps. Shoulders sagged.

But, I said, the ten commandments were being given to a people who had just been led out from a life of enslavement to Egypt. What could this Sabbath commandment mean for them? The class began to see their story in the text.

The Sabbath was a command for all. In this commandment they saw a decree of justice because the Sabbath rest and shalom was for all people, not just the privileged class, as had been their experience. They saw that no one was to be viewed or measured as their position or privilege that day. All were human beings and the playing field was flat. The party was for all. They believed this showed God's true heart for them. Honestly, have you ever read the fourth commandment this way?

They began to bounce out of their seats. "Africa is blessed!" cried one man, "Because see? God loves it." They showed me verses from which they had been taught by the colonists that they were black because they had sinned and needed the white man to rule them. They had believed that their "sin" was why they didn't have work. But through their eyes on the text, the joy and delight of God in the African peoples sprang from the pages. We could have spent the class focusing on the theological and eschatological meaning of the "rest" of God as outlined in my notes, blah de snort. But instead we saw the scriptures come alive and bring freedom and restoration to these people. Their eyes on the text made all the difference.

Seeing through the eyes of the marginalized is not merely a means of administering social justice, though that is important. It is not merely an act of love, though that can hardly be a small thing. The eyes of the marginalized bring to everyone a fullness of understanding in the reading of the biblical text and therefore, to the reading of life. Yes, I learned the tools and rules of hermeneutics in seminary – all about the grammar, rhetoric, genre, historical and cultural contexts, and so forth. But even with such careful study, the biblical text has been used too often to justify horrific events such as slavery, apartheid, oppression of the Native Americans, subjugation of women, and the maltreatment of gays. Seeing through the eyes of the other is crucial to help us to truly hear the Word of God. It is a crucial work in bringing forth the in-breaking of the Kingdom. It is a crucial piece in becoming whom we are meant to be- like Him in this world. We cannot say that we know Truth without the gift of many kinds of eyes to bear witness to the fullness of meaning. We cannot say we know "neighbor" until her eyes become our own.

✝

Ellen Haroutunian is a therapist, spiritual director, writer and urban pastor. She lives in Lakewood, Colorado, with her husband and two retired racing greyhounds.

THIRD WEEK OF LENT:

JOURNEY INTO THE BROKENNESS OF HOMELESSNESS

ENTER THE JOURNEY

> "They will build houses and dwell in them; they will plant vineyards and eat their fruit. No longer will they build houses and others live in them, or plant and others eat" (Isaiah 65:21-22).

> "There are only two families in the world, as my grandmother used to say: the haves and the have-nots."[29]

Begin your weekly meeting by discussing your participation in the $2 challenge. In what ways have you been tempted to take shortcuts over the week to avoid your restricted diet? What long-term impact could it have on your eating habits?

Now try to put yourself in the place of people who are homeless. Homelessness, or house-lessness as it is now often called, is a huge and complex challenge throughout our world. UN-HABITAT's 2005 report indicates that over one billion of the world's six billion residents live in inadequate housing, mostly in the sprawling slums and squatter settlements in developing countries.[30] They estimate that by the year 2050 this figure could rise to over three billion.[31]

In the U.S., an estimated four or five million people go homeless each year. In Australia, an estimated 100,000 people are homeless and in Britain 100,000 households live in temporary accommodation (and are therefore classified as homeless). In every country, the numbers have increased in the last few years, and the fastest growing segment of the homeless population is young women with children. Millions of others live without a safety net and constantly struggle with the knowledge that loss of a job or serious illness could quickly push them onto the streets.

Sit for a few moments and look around your house. Focus on the things you value most—your family photos, the tablecloth lovingly embroidered by your grandmother, the gifts from your mother and father. How would you feel if these were suddenly lost? Even worse, how would you feel if everything else was stripped away too, including your job and your life savings?

Now imagine that you and your family have been forced to travel hundreds of miles to find safety. You are crowded into a makeshift refugee camp with thousands of others. During the trip, your passport and money were stolen. Now you have heard rumors that there is only enough food and water for a small portion of the people in the camp. How would you feel? How would you react? How would you want others to react to you?

Plan some ways to interact with homeless people and refugees each day during the next week. Here are some possible ways to accomplish this:

- Read reflections on homelessness from those who have lived on the streets, like http://thehomelessguy.blogspot.com or http://journeytohomelessness.blogspot.com.
- Find out where the homeless people in your neighborhood congregate and plan a visit.
- Walk around your neighborhood with a friend. Talk to at least one homeless person you encounter and ask them about their life. If possible, find out why they became homeless and why they remain homeless.
- Buy a newspaper from a homeless person when you go shopping.[32]
- Volunteer at a homeless shelter or community for an evening.
- Take a homeless person out for a cup of coffee or for lunch.
- Talk to people who have been refugees. Ask them about their experiences of homelessness.
- Get permission to visit a homeless encampment or refugee settlement if there is one in your area.
- Talk to your church leadership about hosting a homeless encampment (often called a tent city) for a couple of months.
- Plan to spend a night at a homeless shelter or encampment as a sign of solidarity with the homeless.

A Litany for Deliverance from Homelessness

Eternal God, holy and righteous One,
Our world is battered by hurricanes, earthquakes and climate change.
Our lives are drowned by economic downturns and rising food costs.
Our hearts are deluged by uncertain futures and increasing life pressures.
In our pain and anguish, we reach out to you, O God,
Needing the comfort of your love.
We are weary, take our burdens and give us rest.
We are flooded by the many tragedies that fill our world,
Yet we are still thirsty.
We are broken by our fears for tomorrow.
And bowed down by our sorrows.
We share the anxieties of those who have lost their jobs
Our compassion reaches out to those who are homeless,
In our pain and anguish, we reach out to you, O God,
Needing the comfort of your love,
We are weary, take our burdens and give us rest.

Pause to remind yourself of those who live without adequate housing.

God of Hagar and Ishmael,
God of the woman at the well,
God who draws close to those who are outcast and abandoned,
We cry out to you, the One who gives water in the desert,
We trust in you, the One who made a nation from a band of slaves,
We are embraced by you, the One who welcomes us all into the
eternal
family.
God of the despised and rejected ones,
God who gives sons and daughters to those who are alone,
God whose body was broken to bear all grief and carry all sorrow,
We cry out to you, the One who leads us through death into
resurrection,
We trust in you, the One who invites us to drink deeply of the water of
life,
We are embraced by you, the One who welcomes us all into the
eternal
family.

God of mercy and compassion,
God of love and faithfulness,
God who asks us to take up our Cross and follow,
We cry out to you, the One who unveils abundance where we see only scarcity,
We trust in you, the One who makes life flourish in places of death and destruction,
We are embraced by you, the One who welcomes us all into the eternal family.

Read Scripture passages for the day from the Daily Lectionary.

God who was born in a stable because there was no place in the inn,
We believe you still care for all who are homeless and without shelter today.
God who sent Joseph into Egypt to prepare a place for your people,
We believe you still provide for the needs of all who cry out to you.
God who fed the five thousand with a handful of fish and loaves,
We believe you are still able to multiple our efforts and feed all who are empty.
God who asks us not to worry about tomorrow, but to trust in your daily provision,
We believe you still desire to transform our scarcity into your abundance and plenty.
God who sent your son to share our fears and carry our anxieties,
We believe we can give up our burdens and open the floodgates for your mercy and compassion to flow.

Our Father in heaven, hallowed be your name. Your kingdom come, your will be done, on earth as in heaven. Give us today our daily bread. Forgive us our sins, as we forgive those who sin against us. Lead us not into temptation, but deliver us from evil. For the kingdom, the power and the glory are yours, now and for ever. Amen.

God who dwelt on earth with no home to call your own,
Have mercy on all who are homeless and without shelter today.
God, who lives amongst us, hear our prayer.
God who was despised, rejected, and spat upon by those in authority,
Comfort all who are cast by the wayside and ignored today.
God, who lives amongst us, hear our prayer.
God who offers abundance and plenty where we expect scarcity,
Provide for all those who are hungry and in need of food today.
God, who lives amongst us, hear our prayer.

God who promises security and safety when we expect turmoil,
Provide for all those who have lost jobs and are forced into homelessness today.
God, who lives amongst us, hear our prayer.
God who grants us rest in face of our fears and anxieties,
Provide for all those who are anxious about finances today.
God, who lives amongst us, hear our prayer.
God who provides community for all who are alone and abandoned,
Provide for all who feel abandoned and uncared for in these troubled times.
God, who lives amongst us, hear our prayer.
God who is always in control even when nations shake and economies crumble,
Fill all who are empty and rescue those who are enslaved by debt.
God, who lives amongst us, hear our prayer.

Pause to offer your own prayers for the homeless and displaced.

God, you see the unlovely in all of us, yet you still love us. You ask us to reach out with your compassion to all who are unlovely. Open our eyes so that we can see beauty in all people and practice your hospitality, particularly to those homeless and faceless ones who are usually overlooked or ignored by us and by our society.

Lord Jesus Christ, help us to see you in the unlovely faces of those homeless ones the world despises and casts by the wayside. Enable us to reach out with your compassionate embrace so that they too may be welcomed and nursed to wholeness.

May the God who led the people of Israel through the desert
Guard and protect you this day.
May the Christ who transforms the worst experiences into the best of God
Comfort and embrace you this day.
May the Spirit who draws close and seals you with God's love in times of need
Reach into your circumstances and fill you with the water of life.
Amen.

MONDAY

"Home"
Kathy Escobar

i can not for even a minute speak into what it feels like to be without an actual roof over my head. i have always had the luxury and gift of a bed to sleep on, a home to live in, hot water, and food on the table. but, i think there is a homelessness in a physical sense and homelessness in a spiritual and emotional sense. the problem of practical living-life-without-a-roof-over-ones-head is real. the stats are staggering & i believe they will continue to get higher. my dear friends ken & jessica at home-pdx[33] and robbie, matt, nikki & crew at dry bones denver[34] are deeply dedicated to live and love in community with friends who "live outside." they are some of the most powerful examples of incarnational in-the-trenches-love that i have ever seen (and if you ever want to give money to someone, give it to them!)

the refuge community is in the 'burbs, so our issue with homelessness looks different. as you all well know, we are a poor community. we don't have too many two-good-incomes-and-a-high-value-on-giving-away-10%-of-all-that-money-to-help-us-do-this-crazy-thing folks. while none of our friends necessarily live on the streets (maybe in their car now and then), we have many who are continually transient, always behind on rent, never able to catch up, always wandering and never able to get enough stability to really get on their feet. it's an ongoing cycle that without love, support, care, education, and a lot of work will likely continue. we all know that with the current economic state of affairs this population of working poor is only going to grow.

as a friend on the journey, sometimes honestly i feel completely and utterly powerless, helpless, and just-plain-mad at the messed up distribution of resources, not only in the "world" but also in "the church." i know that's a different conversation, but a little like hunger & the issues of food–it is not because the resources aren't there, it's because the resources are not properly distributed. and for us, as christ-followers, it's so worth considering: how can i participate in better redistribution of my current resource? how can we use what we have to help fund, support, encourage actual advocacy & co-housing & food & other very practical things for people who need it? (instead of dumping my money & time & energy in a direction that feeds a machine and not necessarily people.)

one prevailing thought i've had from reading christine sine's lenten reflections was how even though actual physical homelessness might not be prevalent for most of us reading this blog, spiritual/emotional homelessness might be. like the changing economy, we are all aware that there's currently a shifting spiritual landscape. we have a whole crop of folks who "lost their homes" when their faith shifted; what once safely protected them and seemed solid, sure, of durable construction, somehow got ripped off and hurled away, a little like dorothy's house in a wizard of oz. i also think there are so many others out there who grew up in difficult homes where there might have been beds, walls, and a roof, but no sense of belonging and safety. and in the spirit of identifying with Jesus, this is where those of us who are displaced-homeless-exiles-refugees might find a sense of belonging. as he left home & entered into his public ministry, Jesus had "no place to lay his head." but his life was filled with friends and relationships and interactions with crazy people and weird parties and a deep, passionate, intimate connection with God, the Father.

there is a whole desperate world out there, right in our own backyards no matter how rich or poor our neighborhoods might be, that is homeless & yearning for "home." and i think "home" can be created in ways that have nothing to do with 4 walls and a roof:

> home is somehow our hearts being connected to each other in a tangible way.
> home is a relationship that restores dignity & beauty & value where there once was none.
> home is a shared meal and a meaningful conversation about God & life that stirs our
> soul.
> home is the safety of showing the reality of the brokenness in our lives and having people not ditch us.
> home is a shared experience that makes us think.
> home is a desperate hug reciprocated.
> home is a group of people "where everybody knows your name & everybody's glad you came."
> home is a place to bring a small portion of what we have to combine it with other people's small portion and discover that somehow we all leave full.
> home is some weird crazy sense that God is in our hearts and will never leave us,

no matter how dark it gets.

imagine what could happen if the body of Christ spent time building these kinds of homes instead of the ones that require a church consultant and an architect?

Kathy Escobar co-pastors The Refuge, an eclectic faith community dedicated to those on the margins of life and faith. She has written several books, including the most recent, Down We Go: Living Into the Wild Ways of Jesus. *Kathy describes herself as a mommy. wife. friend. pot-stirrer. shepherd. follower of Jesus. peace maker. rule-breaker. dreamer. She lives in Arvada, Colorado, with her husband and five children and blogs regularly about life and faith at kathyescobar.com.*

Tuesday

"Faces of Homelessness"
Ann and Pug Edmonds

Homelessness is not an end in itself. It's a process. It's a life style. It encompasses generations. It holds individuals.

Benjamin chose homelessness. He'd loved Amelia, and they had a daughter. Patiently, and with increasing effort, he attended to diapers, regular meals, family issues. He was a faithful father and took good care of both mother and baby. Then, he left. Now, he lives--for him--comfortably. He has various campsites where he sleeps. He knows every free meal in town and where to go in the rain. With a shy smile on his bearded face, he greets volunteers, other street people, and strangers. He visits Amelia and his daughter, but he lives without responsibility for anyone but himself. Quietly joyful, he exists on the "kindness of strangers."

AnneLise and her two little ones did not chose homelessness. Finally, financial and personal events forced them into sleeping in the car. Kept warm by the car heater and their piles of "blankies," bundles of clothes, and a donated sleeping bag, the three huddle all night in the parking lot or a friend's lent driveway. No chance to do laundry or to take a shower, AnneLise makes sure she and the girls brush their teeth and tidy their clothes each morning. Then, they begin the trek to welfare office, to the employment center, to yet another official place where she files for benefits. Each noon finds them in a free-food place. Each afternoon, the three settle in the children's corner of the library. Often she sneaks a quick sponge bath in the roomy clean bathrooms there. When her gas runs out, she'll have to abandon the car, their current home. Without major and quick intervention, she and the girls will be members of the "on the street" homeless.

The "nearly homeless," like Domingo and his family of six, are a mere paycheck away from loss. He and his wife both work as day laborers in the berry fields, in the motel cleaning crews, and in the landscaping or small construction businesses. Work is not steady. Grandma tends to the three young children. Summer's end brings anxiety as harvests finish and outside work closes down for the season. For two of the children, school starting means two meals a day and a safe place. Food stamps don't cover food needs. Charitable organizations like food banks, clothing exchanges, and church meals help, but it is difficult for the family to get to those without transportation or daylight time. Their apartment is small, crowded with 6. Cutting back on heat, electricity, water, TV makes it seem even grungier. Each week brings another threat. An electricity shut-off notice, a letter from the water company, a requirement from the school for vaccinations. The landlord is no longer willing to accept partial payment for his space. If the rent isn't paid by the 15th, they will be homeless. They will lose their stuff, as they have no way to get it to storage and no money to rent a space for it. Domingo says, "I can only trust in the Lord. Maybe it is a church person helping. Maybe somebody else. Maybe a job starts. Maybe...But the Lord is here for me and for my family. Praise be to God."

Ann and Pug Edmonds live in Bellingham, Washington, and attend St. Paul's Episcopal Church where they coordinate the Alms Ministry. This emergency funding program joins with other faith based organizations to listen to, minister to, and to help homeless and nearly homeless individuals and families. Our Baptismal vows are "to seek and serve Christ in each person" and the Alms Ministry tries to do that.

Wednesday

"Leaving to Find Church"
Ron Cole

For me faith has always been a mystery, a journey over the topography of my mind, heart and soul. It moves me into the broken, and charred pieces of the world around me. So this is where I am. I have left the church, to find the church. Many of my friends do not understand this. They are caught up in Sunday morning…that I have somehow forsaken the assembly of the saints, the singing of spiritual songs, and teaching. Some more critical, that I have lost my way…that I have engaged the slippery slope of losing my faith altogether.

Perhaps, it's best if I give you a glimpse of my church. It begins somewhere around 2:00pm on Sunday afternoon. A group of 3-4 people gather in a small garage in the high Quadra area of Victoria. It's our warehouse where we store our supplies for CARTS. I envision it almost being a sanctuary, because in a sense, it's here we prepare our sacraments for the journey through Victoria's inner city streets. I like the thought of a sacrament being religious symbol or often a offering which conveys divine grace, blessing, or sanctity upon the person who participates in it, or a tangible symbol which represents an intangible reality. Or more, it's the radical scandalous love of God, the redemptive imagination of holiness being justice, and righteousness as God turning the table upside down putting things right in the perspective of his Kingdom.

So what are the sacraments we prepare; it's underwear, men's and women's; it's bags of socks; it's personal packs; it's hats, mitts, gloves and scarves; it's ponchos; bibles; it's fruit, baking, gallons of hot chocolate, sandwiches, cookies, candy.

Some may ask, how are these sacraments? I ask you to let your mind, heart and soul wander into the words of Jesus found in Matthew 25…

> "When I was hungry, you gave me something to eat, and when I was thirsty, you gave me something to drink. When I was a stranger, you welcomed me, and when I was naked, you gave me clothes to wear. When I was sick, you took care of me, and when I was in jail, you visited me."

Then the ones who pleased the Lord will ask, "When did we give you something to eat or drink? When did we welcome you as a stranger or give you clothes to wear or visit you while you were sick or in jail?"

Jesus will answer, "Whenever you did it for any of my people, no matter how unimportant they seemed, you did it for me."

Our service begins, in the vicinity of Queen's and Douglas Street. Anywhere from 8, to 24 people gather to organize, fill and pull carts. This afternoon its about 2 degrees Celsius. The rain is a mix of snow…almost like being hit by a slushy. Across the street we see our friends, our community beginning to gather. They huddle underneath the second floor balcony of Victoria's solution to social housing, the in need of renovation, "Traveller's Inn." Standing at the edge of the intersection, we wait for a gap in the traffic. They wave at us; we return the wave, making a mad dash across in the intersection…CARTS in tow. Immediately, a middle aged first nations woman embraces me, she hugs me, she kisses me on the cheek. Suddenly from now where an image floods my mind…

"But while he was still a long way off, his father saw him and was filled with compassion for him; he ran to his son, threw his arms around him and kissed him." Luke 15:20

I am overwhelmed by love…am I the prodigal son, and this First Nations woman, struggling with addiction, with poverty, with oppression all the injustice in her world. Is she Jesus? I look at her, she looks at me…we laugh.

We give out the clothing, the food, the hot chocolate…and the wet cold rain continues to fall. But there is warmth that is kindled in this community that seems to push away the cold. There is the constant chatter of conversation, sharing stories, smiles, and hugs. They know, and we know, our community is more than just here… that we must move to visit the rest. We say our thanks, our goodbyes and we move along Douglas into the inner city.

We move a few blocks, and underneath the cover of a run down vacant gas station a man sits on the steps working on his bike. He is wet, cold, filthy, and smells…this is the fragrance of broken humanity. This is the incense that attracted Jesus…the offering he found wholly acceptable. We stop to see how he's doing, offer food, a hot drink, socks…a blessings. Our rag tag gang of ragamuffins moves on towards Centennial Square…to the epicenter of Victoria's political power. There again our community has gathered under a covered space below the mayor's office, and council chambers. Again, it is the simplicity of community, conversation, stories, chatter, laughter, hugs, handshakes, pats on the back…there is a profound sense of communion, man and God at table…

"The servant came back and reported this to his master. Then the owner of the house became angry and ordered his servant, 'Go out quickly into the streets and alleys of the town and bring in the poor, the crippled, the blind and the lame.'

Sir,' the servant said, 'what you ordered has been done, but there is still room.

Then the master told his servant, 'Go out to the roads and country lanes and compel them to come in, so that my house will be full.'"

Luke 14:21

To my pleasant surprise, giving out hot chocolate I see a friend I haven't seen since the parking lot behind Capitol Six. He has severe health problems, a constant battle with hepatitis, and HIV. But tonight he is animated, so excited and happy to see us. Again, more hugs and stories, and catching up on all the missing spaces of life.

Just before we leave, we have a prayer circle. I think to myself...this is so ironic. Here we are with Victoria's inner city community, the homeless, the poor, the addicts, the mentally ill. This small circle of seemingly insignificance, of the powerless and the voiceless...huddled under the political power brokers of the city. It is so...Kingdom.

Before we start there is a testimony from the inner city community...he is overwhelmed. He shares about his discovery of Jesus about a year ago. He exudes with joy...tears flow. He tells us of learning how to love people...how much he loves people. Al shares a beautiful prayer of compassion, grace, mercy, love and protection for our friends, our community. There is profound peace, and silence and we move off.

It has been busy here a constant stream of people. Once everyone has got what they need, it's time to move again to Johnson Street to the Salvation Army Shelter. Again they are waiting for us. It is a repeat of the other stops.

Supplies are running low, and the church service is coming to an end. We have one last stop... the "Needle Exchange Van."

We move along Johnson, and in the distance I see a young woman standing at an intersection. The light changes a few times, she does not cross...she does not move. She's waiting...waiting for someone to stop. We arrive at the intersection, she smiles at me, I at her. I know her...I've seen her many times. Another image floods my mind...could she be the prostitute that anointed Jesus feet, and washed them with her tears. I wonder...and am filled with compassion, a profound sense of worship.

We arrive and there is two young men getting crack pipes, and soda. Their eyes brighten up when they see the bananas and cookies we leave at the van. They fill there pockets and love off into the darkness of the night.

We are now back to where we started the church service is over, the van is packed up. In the distance we hear a voice, "Carts,³⁵ is that you?" We have nothing left really. She is living rough on the street…it is wet, and cold. We dig around, we find some polar fleece jackets, some rain gear. She leaves happy that she has something to keep her warm.

Following Jesus has made a profound difference in my faith. My beliefs have changed, my theology has changed. My life, my thinking orbits around the mystery the God-person, Jesus. His divine gravitational pull continues to draw me in. The gospels have become the map in which I navigate life. No matter how many times I read it, in the contours of its topography I am blown away by the redemptive imagination that I continue to find. As dangerous, as wild, as scandalous as the words, as the life of Jesus is…if we dared embrace it, dared live it as Jesus did. I can only imagine…Father your Kingdom come; on earth as in Heaven. As Jesus lived his life, the Kingdom would be here, now.

Following Jesus has taken the leash of my faith, caused me to run wild…church will never be the same for me.

I really dedicate this post to Chris Heuertz, his writing, his passion for Jesus, and his Kingdom have really influenced me over the past few years. Thank you, for words that encouraged me to be bold, to grasp that mustard seed of faith and plant it in the brokenness of my neighborhood.

✛

Ron Cole and his wife Colleen are empty-nesters living on Vancouver Island off Canada's west coast. Ron works as a health care provider as a clinical laboratory technologist in a local hospital. After 20 years working within various ministries in the church, he now finds himself on the fringe. He is a director in CARTS a non-profit organization providing food, clothing and love to the marginalized in Victoria's inner city. Also finds himself regularly in "hot water" in the dish pit of the Rainbow Kitchen, a soup kitchen feeding the working poor, and street community.

THURSDAY

"The Face of Jesus"
Thule Kinnison

The "face" of Jesus doesn't look like the "face" of Jesus...
just ask their name...

As I contemplate Week 3 – Brokenness of Homelessness – This is what is coming up inside of me. I DO have a connection/gift from God that allows me to absolutely feel compassion for the homeless, lost and the sick. I am a recovering drug addict that was addicted for 18 years and have been sober for 5 years now, so my gift of "relating to" has come is the wildest form! As I think of my experiences since I've been sober and following Jesus, with my "friends" (the homeless and addicted) on the streets and encounters with the wanderers and hitch hikers, here's what I remember. I'm blown away when recreating memories of facing Jesus in the flesh in the most awful but really beautiful places in the city of Houston.

When taking food to a homeless guy I've seen on the streets for at least 20 years, who never asks for money or food and is surely mentally challenged and wounded and doesn't talk but mumbles to himself all the time, I asked his name and in the midst of his "mumble" he looks up and says "DAVID" and immediately looks back down, mumbling in "his" language.~ WOW! was my reaction because it seemed like in the midst of his world – he stopped to respond, because I asked.

When I befriended a couple (Brandon and Christina) who lived under the bridge, very addicted to alcohol and crack cocaine, I began to be the hands and feet of Jesus in the midst of chaos, fearlessly! And when Brandon went to jail and went to the hospital, I allowed Christina to stay in my home without restrictions only to find that she really didn't like sleeping inside because the sound of the cars on the overpass is more comforting than the silence of her alone in the house. (we put a fan by her head and left the TV on so she could try to sleep) And at the end of my relationship with them, the church community and I were a part of sending them back home to Denver, Colorado, via Greyhound bus~ I gave Brandon my "Forgiven" necklace before he got on the bus and he put it on and was very proud of it.

When asking the name of a homeless guy I pass by almost every day, I was excited to drive by a few days later and was excited to remember his name and yell out "HI RICK" and what really blew me away is that he said "HI THULE!" (even pronounced it correctly) I was soooo amazed that he actually remembered MY name. What an amazing feeling to just "be known" in that moment. And when I asked "What do you need?" he said "just a towel so I can wash my hair when it gets warmer outside." He didn't want money, food or blankets, just his daily bread… a towel.

I've been given flowers from Hobo Joe Wino Bum who was about 55 years old and is a train hopper – I met him in a store that I was drawn to and had no reason to be in other than hearing God say "go Thule" so I did. He told me about King Solomon and asked why I even talked to him and I said that all people should be known, loved and acknowledged.

I've given my "Cutting Ties for Jesus" bracelet to a young train hopper in downtown who absolutely appeared out of nowhere, as I was thinking to myself "I guess God isn't out here on the streets today."

So really, am I even a part of this world or am I "homeless" as I remember that I will go "home" one day after my visit here?

love, love and then love some more… till the end; or should I say the beginning!

✛

Thule Kinnison is a native Houstonian and mother of two; sober from a 18 year drug addiction; a seeker of deep truth leading the second half of life; a lover and fighter; and, she has an abundance of passion to keep life a mystery. She doesn't know much but what she does know is that she wants to be herself when she grows up.

FRIDAY

"Hollow"
Steve Kimes

O God, I am parched.

I am barely able to move, my need is so deep. Yes, I move in the world, I eat, I drink, I converse. But my body is hollow; my soul is mourning its loss. My God, why have you forsaken us? I already know there is no hope on earth for us.

Why are the needy forsaken? Why do children pick through garbage for food? Why do the simple have no one to support them? Babies hanging on empty breasts; wraith souls brutally violated; men wandering: heartless, hopeless, frenzied, friendless. They cry to you, and pour their hearts to you and they are silenced by death, even while living. Why are the weak only granted more weakness? Why are the mourning gifted ever more sorrow?

And the powerful obtain more power. "Look at my sorrow, observe my need," say those who horde the resources of this world as a toddler who insists that the whole of the world is his own plaything. They offer a drop of water to the desperate and keep an ocean to themselves, never declaring "enough." Why do the sightless insist that compassion is fruitless? Why do the powerful harden their hearts to the helpless?

My God, how do you remain silent? How does heaven remain barred, allowing the foolishly satisfied to claim that all is right in the world? I am starving from your silence. The god-speakers (but not do-gooders) insist that there is peace, peace, yet they do not step outside of their golden palaces long enough to see the sickness, poverty and death. How long will you allow them to speak of your kingdom already come when destruction, despair and disdain reign? How long will you allow them to speak of the miracle of democracy and capitalism, when billions of souls are the cost upon which the society is built? How dare you remain silent! Damn their blasphemies! Entwine their pseudo-god-speak with a millstone and cast them into the deepest lake of fire!

How dare you? How dare you allow these dealers of synthetic theology speak while you remain silent? How dare you allow generation after generation fall while the fat and sassy build themselves up, using your name so casually, so faithlessly? Have you no pride?

But I... my feet come close to stumbling. How easy it is to see a world entombed, and to fail to see the coming consummation. Yours is the power. Yours is the glory. Yours is the kingdom. If only I could enter into your patience. It is so hard to welcome long suffering when children shiver in the cold and are beaten into becoming the next generation of evil-doers. It is difficult to wait.

I know, Lord. I know you have given me everything good. I know that your heart is with the needy. You understand that when your sorrows overwhelm you it is hard to be grateful. You have experienced all of our temptations. I am not thankless, my Father. But we are in need of restoration and resurrection. No economic system, no governmental ideal will grant it to us. Only your love.

We are so parched, my Lord. Satisfy us with your love. Let mercy flood this world, until we drown in it. Allow your compassion to cover our heads, until we cease struggling in its watery depths. Let us finally rest.

Steve Kimes is a pastor among the homeless and the mentally ill in Portland, Oregon. He also has numerous blogs and a website on poverty, theology, philosophy and Jesus.

SATURDAY

"Locked In, But Not Locked Out"
Joy Wilson

I work as a volunteer at Mark Luttrell Correctional Center, a state penitentiary for women in Memphis, Tennessee. One of my favorite opportunities to serve is with Grace Place United Methodist Church, an official UMC church planted in the prison. Grace Place UMC empowers incarcerated women to become disciples of Jesus Christ and experience what it means to be a part of the Body of Christ not only through worship, but service to people in the free world."

Here are women with almost non-existent control over their environment or lives. Those who have jobs make no more than thirty cents an hour, out of which they have to purchase their own toiletries, snacks, stamps, and stationery. The institution tells them when and what to eat, dictates their clothing, options for free time, and access to their families. What can they do to help someone outside the barbed wire fences, and why would they even want to? You might be surprised.

Some of the most humble, committed Jesus-followers I know have life sentences with no parole, but God has transformed their lives, giving them joy and purpose that no prison can take away. They also take Christ's command seriously:

> Then these righteous ones will reply, "Lord, when did we ever see you hungry and feed you? Or thirsty and give you something to drink? Or a stranger and show you hospitality? Or naked and give you clothing? When did we ever see you sick or in prison and visit you?"

> And the King will say, "I tell you the truth, when you did it to one of the least of these my brothers and sisters, you were doing it to me!" (Matthew 25:37-40, NLT)

Wait a minute, that mandate is for people like me, who can decide what to do and where to go, isn't it? Why would the members of Grace Place think this call to action applies to them? Because they know there are people less fortunate than they are who have no certainty of shelter, food, clothing, or medical treatment: the homeless. These incarcerated women have no money to share, but are rich in time and creativity, so that's what they give. For example, those who can crochet make warm hats and shawls with yarn supplied by other churches. They also crochet waterproof sleeping mats using "plarn," which is yarn made from strips of plastic bags looped together.

These inmates may be locked in, but they aren't locked out of ways to follow Jesus, "who came not to serve, but to serve others" Mark 10:45 (NLT). Their actions show the love of Christ to homeless people who, just like them, have no voice in society. Both long for justice: being treated with the respect and dignity they are often denied. And I'm a part in this chain of compassion as a prison ministry volunteer, sharing the love of Jesus that dominoed down to me.

Each of us has a unique place in God's universe. We are made in His/Her image to fulfill a special part for the redemption of us all. God loved us into being, and when we pass that love along to someone else, we are literally the hands, feet and heart of Jesus and have the transformational power to change someone's life for the better. Just like God did for us. Just like someone in our lifetime did for us.

Does what we do make any real difference when we act with kindness, giving what we want for ourselves?

Ask the women of Grace Place and people who sleep under a bridge.

Joy Wilson is the author of Uncensored Prayer: The Spiritual Practice of Wrestling with God. *She has a passion for prison ministry, and is an advocate for middle-aged and senior women, and anyone who suffers from depression. Visit Joy at joyleewilson@gmail.com.*

Fourth Week of Lent:

Journey into the Brokenness of Creation

Enter the Journey

According to the Global Footprint Network, if everyone lived like Americans, we would need almost five and a half planets to sustain us. If we lived like Canadians or Australians or Brits we would need four planets to sustain us. Bangladesh has the lightest footprint—if we all lived at the level of the average Bangladeshi the earth would support 22 billion people.

It is not only our level of consumption that determines the ecological footprint, however. Italy's eco-footprint is two-thirds that of other European countries, because Italians eat less processed food. Eating fresh rather than processed food (particularly processed meat and dairy) could immediately shrink your environmental footprint.

If every UK household installed 3 compact fluorescent light bulbs, enough energy would be saved in a year to supply all street lighting in the country. Five hundred billion to 1 trillion plastic bags are used worldwide each year, which is 150 bags for every person on earth.

"You care for the land and water it; you enrich it abundantly. The streams of God are filled with water to provide the people with grain, for so you have ordained it" (Psalm 65:9).

Begin your weekly meeting by discussing your discipline for the past week. How did talking to homeless people make you feel? What new insights did it give you into their way of life? In what ways have you been tempted to take shortcuts over the week to avoid or minimize your interaction with the homeless? Discuss ways you could interact with the homeless on a long-term basis.

Now focus on your new discipline. Check out the impact that your way of life has on the environment. Measure your own eco-footprint. If you have internet access, get each person to do the eco-footprint quiz at http://footprintnetwork.org. If internet access is not available, suggest that participants check out their eco-footprint before they attend. What was your immediate reaction to this information? Were you shocked by your consumption and its impact on the world? Discuss ways that you would like to simplify your life during this next week in order to decrease your impact on the earth.

Here are some suggestions that you could commit to for the week
- Use public transport or carpool rather than drive your own car to work each day.
- If public transport is not available, plan a car-free day for you and your family.
- Purchase reusable shopping bags (canvas or biodegradable material) and begin using them for your grocery shopping.
- Replace all of the incandescent lights in your house with new compact fluorescent lights (CFLs) or halogens, both of which use significantly less energy and also last many years more.
- Replace your coffee and tea with fair-trade brands. Find out where you can buy other fair-trade food items in your neighborhood
- Visit the local farmers market and use only produce that comes from the market.
- Send a note of thanks to local organic farmers as a sign of appreciation for their efforts to preserve God's creation while providing food for your table.
- Take a special lunch to migrant farm workers on a local farm. They often do backbreaking work for little pay.
- Buy local. When purchasing items this week, consider the distance they had to travel in order to reach you and the amount of petroleum used in the process. Whether in the grocery or hardware store, factor the proximity of the source into your purchasing criteria.
- Enjoy the 100 Mile Diet[36] for a week. Only consume food that has been grown within one hundred miles of your home.

A Litany for the Restoration of Creation

God of wind and storm,
God of trees and flowers,
God of birds and beasts,
God of men and women,
God you gave birth to all creation,
Yet now it groans, devastated, polluted and cut down.

Take a moment to visualize a place you know that is polluted, imagine in your mind what its restoration would do.

God, all of created life groans waiting for the future you are bringing into being.
It waits in painful longing for restoration and renewal.
We hope for the day on which all you have made will be rescued from death and decay,
We wait for the redemption of our bodies and the restoration of our world.

> In my opinion whatever we may have to go through now is less than nothing compared with the magnificent future God has planned for us. The whole creation is on tiptoe to see the wonderful sight of the sons of God coming into their own. The world of creation cannot as yet see reality, not because it chooses to be blind, but because in God's purpose it has been so limited – yet it has been given hope. And the hope is that in the end the whole of created life will be rescued from the tyranny of change and decay, and have its share in that magnificent liberty which can only belong to the children of God!

> It is plain to anyone with eyes to see that at the present time all created life groans in a sort of universal travail. And it is plain, too, that we who have a foretaste of the Spirit are in a state of painful tension, while we wait for that redemption of our bodies which will mean that at last we have realized our full sonship in him. We were saved by this hope, but in our moments of impatience let us remember that hope always means waiting for something that we haven't yet got. But if we hope for something we cannot see, then we must settle down to wait for it in patience.[37]

God, in this season of hope and promise,
bless the earth rich and fertile with life.
God, in this season of planting and growth,
bless the seed we plant and nurture.
As it falls into the ground to grow
may we remember your body broken for us.

> Unless a seed is planted in the soil and dies it remains alone
> But its death will produce many new seeds,
> a plentiful harvest of new lives.[38]

God, as we sprinkle our gardens with the water that gives life,
Let us remember lands that are parched and those that are flooded.
God, as we hike our favourite trails and enjoy our favourite vistas,
Let us remember forests that are cut down and soils that are polluted.
God, as we play with our pets and enjoy their company,
Let us remember animals slaughtered and species extinct.

Lord Jesus Christ, may we remember,
that your life blood was poured out for us,
You were hung upon a tree and crucified,
So that together with all your creation,
we might be liberated into freedom.

> Open up, O heavens, and pour out your righteousness
> Let the earth open wide
> So salvation and righteousness can sprout up together.[39]

As we watch for the first sprouts of new creation,
We remember your resurrection promise.
A new world is breaking into ours with abundance and wholeness,
Polluted waters are being restored,
Endangered species are being protected,
Devastated forests are being replanted.

> Look, I am making all things new…
> On each side of the river grew a tree of life
> Bearing twelve crops of fruit with a fresh crop each month
> The leaves were used for medicine to heal the nations.[40]

Christ, we wait for your resurrection life to be seen in its fullness,

We wait for your healing be revealed in our bodies.
We wait for your healing power be seen in the soil,
We wait for your healing power to be seen throughout the earth.
Come, Lord Jesus
Let us participate together in the coming of a new heaven and a new earth.
Amen.

MONDAY

"The Spiritual Discipline of Creation Care"
Geoff and Sherry Maddock

Next door to our home, our urban farm is alive with bees hovering, fruit trees growing strong, blackberries creeping up fence-posts, and watermelons expanding like balloons among the bright marigolds. While these are all beautiful to behold, we have new favorite subjects inhabiting this tenth of an acre lot. Two weeks ago nine 12-week-old chickens were delivered: four bold Barred Rocks and five regal Araucanas. These delightful birds are quickly making themselves at home in their new coop, and we eagerly anticipate them providing us with some hyper-local eggs in due course.

While we are excited about enjoying the edible bounty of our urban farm (honey, fruit, vegetables, and eggs), we are also mindful that caring for the land and its creatures works to form us into certain kinds of people. The true fruit arrives as our lives are transformed. We observe the variety of seeds, the tender seedleaf pushing up through the soil, and the first signs of productivity in a mature plant. We also become students of those marvelous chickens—their likes and dislikes, their rest and their play—and in turn we become better disciples of our Creator God.

Caring for animals forms us in a way that no other spiritual disciple can because when we were first made, we were created to share a garden with fellow creatures – human and non-human – and our Creator God. This trinity of relationships – God, Humans, Created-world – is where wholeness can finally be found in a world that's is torn at the seams by sin. To care for a piece of land – no matter how small – and steward animals is to see brokenness and redemption up close. Plants and animals get sick and die. Weeds invade the earth and pests destroy new life. Seasons come and go imparting blessings and challenges. We also observe animals recovering from sickness and playing again with renewed vigor. We watch as destructive aphids become breakfast for lady beetle larva. When we turn our attention to the created world and its creatures, we will find a way forward into some of the deepest truths of the Creator.

The writer of Proverbs esteems wisdom as the highest goal for humans and in this regard, draws our attention to creation (creature!) care: "The wise know the needs of their animals" (Proverbs 12:10). Job points out that animals direct our attention to the Creator. He argues against the apparent wisdom of his friends and for the genius of the "animals, plants, and fish" who, "teach, tell, and declare" the truth about God's ways (Job 12:7-10). Last, but certainly not least, Jesus likens his own love and self-sacrifice to that of a mother hen (Luke 13:34). As we steward these chickens and other creatures in our care we discover an ironic truth. We can only reach our full, God-defined humanity as we humbly give our concern and attention to the other creatures God has made. All the theory in the world will not make us Christ like. If we are to truly be sons and daughters of the most-high God, we will need to get our hands dirty and become humble stewards of God's loving handiwork.

Gardens give us the place to do this stewardship work and they echo the truth and beauty of that first garden described in Genesis. At the same time, gardens call us forward to when heaven and earth will overlap and interlock in the garden city of Revelation. In this season of Lent we are mindful of the olive orchard of betrayal and arrest, the garden tomb, and the first fruits of New Creation. The wholeness we long for involves more than just personal healing – biblical wholeness is placed. Only when we inhabit the place around us as stewards can we hope to enter into the delights of being fully human.

So, we watch our new neighbors in the chicken run. We watch carefully for the brave ones, the skittish ones, and the ones that are first to race toward a fresh bucket of kitchen scraps. We watch with the expectation that we will discover more about the character and love of our Creator God and that we will be transformed into the true humanity Jesus modeled for us.

Geoff and Sherry Maddock, along with their 10-year-old-son Isaac, make their home in downtown Lexington, Kentucky. They work as missionaries to cultivate beauty, food, and neighborliness on their 1/10th of an acre urban farm and take great inspiration from the God who makes and renews chickens, bees, fruits trees, and soil.

TUESDAY

"Our Industrial Wound and the Salty Tears of God"
Jason Fowler

I was deeply troubled by the 2006 Gulf of Mexico BP oil spill, which we should more appropriately call an oil eruption. I'm not sure the media was even free to report on the profound proportions of this incident. It was not merely an environmental catastrophe of epic scale- it was something more- and the nature of this cataclysm is yet to be seen.

This event caused widespread emotional reactions across the country and especially in the Gulf Coast- which rightly it should. There was grief, as images of wildlife and birds mired in thick oil have hit the media. There was rage and calls for BP to be taken to the economic gallows and hung for its atrocities. There was shock as many who depended on the Gulf for their livelihoods in effect became servants of the cleanup, possibly never again to fish the toxic waters. There was frustration as government officials and corporate CEOs bought more time with strong words and weak-willed actions. And there was lament - an awareness that somehow we are part of the economic-growth-obsessed suicidal system that produced this disaster.[41]

In the midst of all these many reactions though, I believe we have a fundamental misunderstanding as to what this event signified. And when I say signify, I mean-what does this event mean? What does this event say about the state of our hyper-consuming country and the industrial world- and even the position of our own uncomfortably troubled souls? It would be easy to say it signifies nothing, that it is just another terrible event- or worse- bad news that we just can't stomach for another day. I understand this response- but I think this reaction speaks volumes of our addiction to...not oil, but...denial. We can only take so much bad news. But I'm not sure why we think we should try to insulate ourselves as much as possible from a troubled world.

Sometimes I think the real folks who are in need of help are those of us trapped in our air-conditioned homes and gated communities. We have lost our ability to creatively engage, by the Holy Spirit, a sin-sick world. We are weary of having to process the 'bad news out there,' and in reality we would rather remain a disembodied, disengaged consumer of mostly more positive 'virtual' experiences and information- but therein lies our brokenness (and my own included).

Despite our desire to forget the 'bad news' in the Gulf though, the ramifications will most likely go on for generations. This is not something that is going away anytime soon. If we are loving we will respond in whatever ways we can to help the communities most affected. If we are wise we will realize that this environmental disaster was a mirror or a window into the ways we've chosen to live- a lifestyle that on one end produces efficiency and convenience-an endless amount of pleasures and delights- and on the other end produces a never-ending stream of toxic waste, disease, and ecological breakdown which multiplies social and economic crisis in the communities surrounding the exit or entry points of our production systems (near factories, factory farms, energy plants, landfills, etc). Unfortunately, the latter end is hidden from our sight behind barbed wire fences, factory walls, deceptions, and even our own bodies. We only feel the sting of the consequences when the system fails to hide the effects or when the cycle of consequence reaches maturity through events of crisis, whether through our own ill health, the destruction of GOD's creation in our immediate or regional locality (and beyond), or other means.

It is crucial for us to remember that the broken BP oil well is not an anomaly in the modern world. This kind of devastation may not happen every day in the Gulf (at least not on this scale), but certainly it is undeniable by now that the fouling of our lands, waterways and air is a typical by-product of the assembly line, the power plant, of the landfill – which in turn are the engines behind the very lifestyle we have become comfortable with and accustomed to. We are caught in a web that we have learned to love while we deny the possibility of living beyond it. After all, who would want to give up a life of comfort and ease? If there was no factory where would I get all that I need to live? If there was no power plant where would I get the electricity I need to live? If there was no factory farm where would I get the food I need to live? If there was no landfill where would I put all the trash that I produce? For most of us we have fully and willingly resigned ourselves to this fate. For others of us, our economic troubles mean we can't live beyond the web because we're too busy surviving- there is no time to consider long term consequence- or so we think.

What has happened in the Gulf is no mere oil spill. It is not an accident in the truest sense of the word; it is an open wound. It is the lifeblood of the Industrial Age mixing with the salty tears of GOD. It is a wound we have inflicted on ourselves. It is the howling of creation as it stands betrayed by its caretakers. And what will be our response? What will be our course into the future? Two roads stand before us. One leads to further pain- it is paved with human pride and self-centered ingenuity. The other road is paved with humility and a crying out to GOD to teach us how live in His love and wisdom and abundance that surrounds us (and from there will spring our ingenuity).

Can we attain a measure of 'societal salvation' if we return to a pre-industrial way of life or pursue a new age of renewable energies (which some of which I am for)? Is a life free of oil or electricity really more righteous or redemptive? Can carbon trading, nuclear power plants, wind farms and seas of solar panels really redeem us from our ways? The answer is no because the deeper issue is the inner destructiveness of our fragmented souls. Environmental issues are exposing our spiritual deadness before the Creator of All Things. There is but one remedy-one catalyst for true and lasting change- and that is to be first and foremost reconciled, through Jesus, with our Creator. Our future lies in humility before GOD and not in our utopian dreams. From that point of reconciliation a new way of life can begin.

Jason Fowler is the co-founder, along with his wife Pam, of Sustainable Traditions - a project that calls for the renewal of an embodied, holistic pursuit of Jesus and His kingdom in the context of intentional living. He lives on a farm near the Blue Ridge Mountains of Virginia.

WEDNESDAY

"Sabbath and Sea Creatures"
Jeremiah Griffin

Sabbath—the practice of intentionality, rest, and reflection that Christians inherited from Judaism-- is presented with seemingly conflicted views in the Bible. In Isaiah 58:9b-14 we learn that if we refrain from trampling on the Sabbath, from pursuing our own interests on God's holy day, then we will learn to take delight in the Lord and our lives will be like a watered garden, whose springs never fail. Yet in Luke 13:10-17, Jesus' actions cause us to wonder whether or not he supports keeping Sabbath laws.

Unsurprisingly, today's Christians seem collectively stumped by the confusion surrounding this gift we've inherited. And as such, we've allowed it to fall into disrepair. Like weeds in an overgrown garden, pressures for productivity and busyness have crept in, leaving our lives overcrowded and unmanageable. What is Jesus communicating to us today? What is the deeper discipline of Sabbath?

Not long ago I heard the story of a woman named Sylvia Earle. Now 78 years old, Sylvia spent most of her career working as an oceanographer, studying the mysteries that lie hidden beneath the veil we call sea level. During a time when much attention was turned skywards for the Moon landing, Sylvia plumbed the depths of inner-space to discover a jungle of life right beneath our noses.

Slyvia's peers know her as "Her Deepness," a title she earned by leading the first team of women aquanauts on a dive to over 1,200 feet below sea level. There, with the aid of a small submarine trailing behind her and a now antiquated diving suit, she walked with her own two feet on the ocean floor. Her exploration lasted for over two and a half hours—about the same amount of time that Buzz Aldren spent on the Moon—but few noticed.

In that vast subterranean wilderness, Sylvia found herself surrounded by tall plants in the dark currents that shimmered with bio-luminescent light. There were crabs and fish of all shapes, colors, and sizes. She saw creatures barely describable as creatures and patches of sand that glowed when touched. After some time, she ordered the submarine to turn off its lights, so she could be fully immersed in the wonders that surrounded her.

In many ways Sabbath can be likened to her journey, for it teaches us the importance of exploring those hidden, rarely visited corners of life—of listening for the still, small Voice. With all the noise of today's continuous stimulation (from radios, TVs, bills, and trying to stay on top of email), rare is the person who feels they can take time away for renewal. But our spiritual... and even physical health... demands this. And like Sylvia turning off the submarine lights, taking such time gives us a chance to pause and bask in God's goodness—a time to grow still, love those we cherish, and nurture a quiet awareness of God's presence.

When Sylvia reflects back on her life, she's quick to point out how much has changed. Creatures never before fathomed have been brought to light. The earth's resources have been used in new and exciting ways, transforming life as we know it. But what began with perhaps limitless optimism, has given way to myriad unanticipated problems.

Now, when people ask Sylvia where she would go diving, if she could go anywhere in the world, she answers, "Oh... just about any place... 50 years ago." She says this because of all the damage that's recently happened to underwater ecosystems. Many species of ocean creatures have been reduced to five or ten percent of what they once were... and some have been fully eradicated. Apparently, for instance, Galveston, Texas, used to have Monk Seals, a species that once stretched from here to Florida. But the last Gulf Coast Seal was seen in 1952.

This highlights another facet of Sabbath—the need to exercise restraint. Failure to set limits, by allowing time for rest and replenishment, reliably precedes burnout. God modeled rest for us on the seventh day of creation, and Israel received the Sabbath as a gift, after being freed from slavery—hard things to argue against.

So why then does Jesus wind up squaring off with the synagogue leader in the Gospel of Luke? Was Jesus really opposed to Sabbath? Well, if we revisit the story, we notice that the woman who was bent over didn't come to Jesus. She didn't interrupt his teaching. She lurked quietly within the crowd and had Jesus not called out to her, she would have left unnoticed. But that's not what happens —because Jesus had a point to make.

Now, the voice opposing Jesus was correct in saying that he could have waited until the next day to heal the woman. After all, she'd already been waiting for eighteen years. But, by moving to heal her anyway, Jesus makes a theological point about Sabbath's purpose. In the Message translation, Jesus responds, "You frauds. Each Sabbath every one of you regularly unties your cow or donkey from its stall. You lead it out for water and think nothing of it. Why then would it be wrong for me to untie this daughter of Abraham and lead her from the stall where Satan has kept her bound?"

You see, Sabbath is about more than rest and renewal… it's also about freedom from bondage—about grace and healing. Its rules and commandments ought to be subordinate to the greater purpose they serve—that of freeing us to walk in a fuller awareness of God's presence and provision. Or as Jesus says in Mark, "Sabbath was made for humankind, and not humankind for the Sabbath."

So God's chief concern, made known by Jesus, is the full and unhindered flourishing of all life. But, as Sylvia and others point out, the need for Sabbath extends beyond humanity to the whole of God's creation. Soil needs rest for the replenishment of nutrients. Groundwater needs time to recover. And when resources are overtaxed, they wither and dry up. But we do likewise.

And, in this way, we mirror today's ecological predicament. Today's endless chase for outward economic gain comes at a cost. We find ourselves held captive by a society that expects ever longer working hours—where families are strained and relationships sacrificed. A contagious hunger to prosper or have the greatest, most respected credentials has left us scattered and depleted. Even our self-images have fallen prey, for we never feel free to simply rest. There's always more that can be done.

Let us then cherish the gifts we've been given and, like Sylvia's dazzling walk at the bottom of the sea, allow Sabbath to open up new horizons of wonderment. But we must be willing to dive deep—to clear space with intentionality. Because like tithing and loving our enemies, Sabbath requires discipline. But as Jesus reminds us, our reward can be walking in the perfect freedom God wills for us, with an ever-increasing awareness of God's presence in all things!

Rev. Jeremiah C. Griffin serves at Trinity Episcopal Church in Galveston, Texas and as the Executive Director of the William Temple Episcopal Center, a student ministry of the Episcopal Diocese of Texas. He is passionate about matters concerning ecology and faith and spends much of his free time exploring nearby coastal lands with his family.

Thursday

"Lessons from the Garden"
Christine Sine

Gardening is an important part of the rhythm of my life. I have always loved God's creation, but it is only since I settled in Seattle that I have become an avid gardener. As part of our commitment to simplicity and self-sustainability, we grow as much of our own fruits and vegetables as possible on our urban lot. Fortunately the climate in the Pacific Northwest is ideal for this venture. At this time of the year, our front porch bulges with seedlings ready to be planted. I know of no more satisfying experience than to eat produce freshly harvested and cooked from the garden.

Celebrating God's presence in the garden is one way I absorb the soothing rhythms encased in the seasons of the year. Early monastic communities recognized gardening as part of God's mandate to care for the Earth and believed gardens enabled them to re-create the paradise man and woman once shared with God.

Gardening not only renews and refreshes me; it has also taught me important lessons about our Creator God. In her book *Looking For God*, Nancy Ortberg says, "Nature holds more beauty than our eyes can bear,"[42] which beautifully sums up why I have developed such a love affair with the garden. We can try to re-create an experience of heaven in our churches with bells, smells, and rich ornamentation, but that doesn't come close to the wonder of God experienced in the fragrance of flowers, the melody of birdsong, and the beauty of plants and animals.

I think that one reason people are moving away from Christianity at time-warp speed is because we have so divorced our faith from the natural world. We confine our worship to a small, stuffy church building and restrict our devotion to reading words about God without connecting to the glory of God all around us. I read about the death and resurrection of Christ in the Bible, but I experience it every time I plant a seed and watch it burst into life. I read about the faithfulness of God to Israel, but I experience it every time I watch the rain fall and nourish the seeds I have planted. I read about the miracle of the fish and the loaves, but I experience a miracle every time I am overwhelmed by the generosity of God's harvest.

Gardening has also taught me to pay attention to the beauty, diversity, and creativity of God's world. As I watch the days and the seasons follow in their expected patterns, I am reminded of the faithfulness of a God who comes to us in all seasons of our lives. I am also reminded that our God, who poured out his great love in the complexity, beauty, and diversity of creation, still cares for us and for all creation and will never abandon what he has made.

Probably my most profound garden lessons come from winter. Why, I wonder, do we prune our fruit trees in the winter when they seem so bare and vulnerable? Or probably more to the point, why does God insist on pruning our lives during the difficult winters of suffering that all of us endure? Winter pruning encourages roots to go down deeper and strengthen the tree. The harder we prune, the more vigorous the spring growth will be and the greater the harvest. Maybe it is the same in our lives; God often prunes us during the frigid seasons of struggle and pain, when the branches seem bare and our souls feel most vulnerable. And often the pruning is just as severe as what I inflict on my trees. If we really want to be fruitful during the seasons of harvest that God allows us, then we need to be willing to be pruned and shaped not during the times that life is good when we can handle a little painful cutting, but during those wintery season when we feel spring will never come again.

Perhaps you don't enjoy gardening like I do, but as we move into the summer and the rich abundant harvest of God's provision, you may like to spend time thinking about how God reveals himself to you through creation. In particular, think about and pray for those who earn their living through interaction with God's creation. Farmers, forestry workers, landscape gardeners, and conservationists are but a few of the professions that labor in God's creation who need our prayers. We all reap the benefits of their efforts as we eat their produce, admire their landscapes, and walk amongst the parks they preserve.

The wonder and glory of God is all around us. May we all open our eyes to see and experience God in new ways this season.

Christine Sine is the Executive Director of Mustard Seed Associates. She trained as a physician in Australia and developed the medical ministry for Mercy Ships. She now speaks on issues relating to changing our timestyles and lifestyles to develop a more spiritual rhythm for life. She has authored several books including Return to Our Senses: Reimagining How We Pray; Godspace: Time for Peace in the Rhythms of Life; *and* Tales of a Seasick Doctor. *Christine blogs at http:// godspace-msa.com.*

Friday

"Composting as a Spiritual Practice"
Steve Taylor

In recent weeks I've been enjoying the spiritual practice of composting.

As with most spiritual practices, it has been a mix of great fun and hard work, pulling on the gumboots and old jersey, lugging around big bags of animal manure, tossing straw, shoveling and raking.

For me, making compost has become a spiritual practice that connects me with God and helps me pray.

As I compost, I think about my local community and people who are not yet in faith. I recall the people I know who are really struggling with life. I think back over the TV news, holding before God, the life situations that seem bleak and barren.

I wonder if composting was part of what God was doing in Genesis 2. The story describes God planting a garden. Given the detail, the slow and careful pace in the Bible narrative, there is this sense of the garden taking time, sort of evolving. God is the careful composter, mixing love with manure, compassion with planting, dreams of fruitful relationship as life is blown in human nostrils. Reading Genesis 2 has begun to turn my act for composting into a spiritual practice, an act of communion with Gardener of the Universe.

1 Corinthians 13 reminds us that these three remain: faith, hope and love.

Composting is an act of faith. You place compost on the garden in autumn. You let it sit over the winter, with an occasional turn and toss. And come spring, newly planted vegetables will be growing green and I'll be preparing to say "Thank you very much" over a summer salad.

So I compost in faith, that in darkness and amid the muck, things might yet grow. As I compost, I am reminded that new life, indeed, all life, is out of my control, beyond my action, logic or planning.

Composting is an act of hope. I affirms that in the very midst of autumn decay, through the bleak breakdown of winter, things might get grow, that death is never the end of the story, that confusion and chaos, are simply the raw material for a fresh start.

Composting is a prayerful act of love. To care for the soil becomes for me a practice both of loving God's earth and prayerfully caring for people. In the peace of my garden I let go, offering people and places to God, inviting God's power into the dark places of the world.

Composting. It has become a spiritual practice that connects me in prayer with God and my world.

Steve Taylor is married to Lynne and together we enjoy two daughters, Shannon and Kayli Anne. To relax I enjoy pub music, coffee, reading and wine (Kiwi whites and Australian reds). My initial work was in the orchards of Central Otago, New Zealand. From a background in horticulture, I became fascinated by growing people and healthy communities as well as plants. I have planted a church in Auckland, pastored in Christchurch, and am currently the principal of Uniting College for Leadership and Theology in Adelaide, South Australia.

Saturday

"We Pray, Redemption Happens"
Michael Carroccino

There is a tribe in the desert southwest of the U.S. that claims responsibility for the world's rain: they believe it is their prayers which bring rain for the whole earth. It matters not whether the rest of us agree, nor whether we participate – theirs is a higher calling than any opinion poll or public service campaign. They pray; rain happens. This lends a surreal gravity to their ritual and prayers, and – at their best – they will use the rest of their daily activities to keep them in good shape for that central part of their tribal identity. Like most southwestern tribes, they offer cornmeal to the wind as they pray – a powder that represents the whole of their year's labor, the livelihood of their community and their bodies. It blows away from their hands to be returned to the soil and to the birds; to become life for the next cycle of seasons.

What do we offer with our lives? By this I don't mean the spiritual offering our prayer so much as I mean the physical remains of our day-to-day living. Late industrial manufacturing has given us the unfortunately accurate term "throughput" to refer to the stuff we make and use on a regular basis. The trouble with throughput is that it doesn't really imply a cycle so much as a one-way trajectory – the truth of which I observe each week as I leave my trash by the curb – or each time I take another round of items to donate or 'recycle.' Our world seems to be based upon a system whereby we remove material from our planet and make it unusable – even toxic – before returning it to hermetically sealed holes in which we desperately hope it will remain harmlessly isolated from the surrounding environment. We put the essence of our labor in landfills, and we pray it does not irreversibly contaminate the next cycle of seasons.

The documentary film *Manufactured Landscapes* (2006) tells the story of photographer Edward Burtynsky, who stumbled upon his calling when he took a wrong turn one day and came upon a surreal – and disturbing – landscape of mine tailings feeding into a noxious fluorescent creek bed. As he set up his camera, he began to contemplate how the landscapes that surround the large-scale manufacturing required to maintain our style of living reflect a fundamental disconnect between modern visions of 'the good life' and basic care for the earth and the workers that produce the various bits and pieces of such a life. From there, he began to travel the world, finding story after story etched in the landscapes of our society that reflect the unconscious resolve in our culture to ignore the full cycle of manufacturing implicit in our choices and attitudes about consumption.

The scale of Burtynsky's photographs dwarfs our capacity to imagine our own impact on the planet, and the accompanying videography adds an element of time and progress that only sharpens this display of the dystopian reality that we live in. Whether panning through a seemingly endless factory where countless workers bend quietly over tables assembling blender motors at breakneck speed, visiting a rural village filled with mounds of imported electronic waste, or looking at a tremendous photographic rendering of the gargantuan maw of an abandoned granite quarry, we who view these works are left with indelible images of the not-so-subtle cruelties that our daily choices inflict around the globe. What's more, we are left with an acute sense of powerlessness – a despair that such a system can ever be stopped – or perhaps even slowed – before it reaches a predictable end.

The spiritual message of our industrialized world is an addicted cry of "fill me, fill me!" while we work with great energy to despoil all that which sustains us. This reality is an outgrowth of what I see as our world's approach to body and soul: we are taught in a thousand ways to see our bodies, our spirits, as resources to be mined, as assets that we can tap for personal gain in our endless quest to be satiated from the discomfort of the reality of being human. Those holes that we leave in our planet are the sacrament – the outward and visible sign – of the collective sickness of our spirits. Until we learn as a people to cultivate our own sense of God's clear-eyed compassion upon the brokenness of our human world, the holes – the poison – will continue to manifest from our deepest selves; our prayers will bring no rain.

What do we offer, then? What can we offer? Simply: ourselves, our souls and bodies. Each time Christians make prayers together, we are doing so as God's eternal priesthood of believers. We believe that – no matter whether others agree or participate – our Eucharistic prayer brings redemption upon the whole world. The redemption piece is God's, the offering is ours. We make offerings of bread and wine and money – which become the food for the next round of prayer and giving, service and ministry. Our offerings become ourselves, they become our community. When we put money in the plate, it signifies the sum total of our labor – it is our offering to God that we pray will be transformed upon the altar into redemption for the world. Like our native kin, let us focus then upon keeping that vision through the other six days – let us use all of our daily activities to keep us in shape for this most central part of our identity. With practice and with time, our offerings can be transformed – to become life for the next cycle of seasons. We pray, redemption happens.

✛

Michael Carroccino loves spending time outdoors with his family in the mountains and islands of western Washington. He has been at various times a carpenter, an Episcopal priest, and a canyoneering guide.

FIFTH WEEK OF LENT:

Journey into the Brokenness of God's Family

ENTER THE JOURNEY

> "Americans by and large work together, shop together, and play together, but they do not worship together. If we are at our core spiritual, then the fact that we seem unable and unwilling to relate to one another elbow-to-elbow in the pews of the local congregation reveals how fragile the integrity of the church is."[43]

It has been said that Sunday morning is the most segregated time in our Christian life. We are segregated by race, age, economic class, denominational affiliation, and theological perspectives. We gravitate towards those who think and worship in the same way we do. Often, instead of living together in unity and love, we are separated by prejudice and intolerance.

Yet the golden rule of Christianity, what James calls "the royal law," is "love your neighbor as you do yourself."[44]   At a recent conference, Pakistani theologian Charles Amjad Ali reminded us that we are all prejudiced. What changes in dialogue with others is the focus of our prejudice. He then challenged us to consider, "Can we be prejudiced towards justice, equality, and respect, or do we always live primarily with the prejudices of exclusion?"

God is much bigger than our culturally bound viewpoint. All people are created in God's image and worthy of being treated with respect and understanding. I do not believe that we will fully understand who God is or appreciate the incredible sacrifice of Christ on the Cross until we learn to see these events through the eyes of others who come from very different viewpoints than our own.

> "How good and how pleasant it is when God's people live together in unity!" (Psalm 133:1).

Begin your weekly meeting by discussing your discipline from the past week. What was the most challenging aspect of your week? What new insights did you gain regarding your use of the earth's resources? In what ways have you been tempted to take shortcuts over the week and rationalized your use of resources? What permanent changes are you considering making in your life in order to reduce your impact on the earth?

Now focus on your new discipline for the upcoming week. Discuss your prejudices. What ethnic and religious groups do you struggle to understand? Of what theological viewpoints are you intolerant? What other prejudices separate you from God's people. Talk about ways to bridge the gap between these different groups during this week.

Here are some suggestions that you might like to consider. In each situation ask yourself: What are the life experiences that have molded their view of faith? Where do you have beliefs in common? What are the differences? What are the foundations for unity and respect?

- Plan to get together with someone in your church who has a different theological perspective than your own. Make this specifically a time to listen to their ideas and learn from their understanding of faith.
- Visit a church of another denomination or worship style that you have never been a part of before.
- Visit a church from a different ethnic background that you are unfamiliar with. Visit their web and check out the theological discussions of indigenous peoples in country.

A LITANY FOR UNITY IN THE CHURCH

God who is One, you call us to be one,
May we be one with all who are made in your image.
God who is three, you call us to be community,
May we find community with all who are called by your name.
God may many hearts become one in you,
May we all be knit together in unity and common purpose.

Pause to remind yourself of the rich diversity of Christ's body.

God almighty, today by the power of your spirit we unite in prayer,
We unite with all our sisters and brothers in your worldwide community.
We unite with sisters and brothers from all churches and denominations,
We unite with all who are joined by the holy spirit of God.
We unite with followers from every church and congregation,
We unite with God's daughters and sons from every creed and culture.

Read Scripture passages for the day from the Daily Lectionary.

God, today we believe that you dwell in all who confess Jesus as the Son of God,
God, today we will open our ears to listen attentively to each one who confesses Jesus as the Son of God.
God, we believe you invite us to accept each other as sisters and brothers,
God, today we accept and embrace all who call themselves by your name.
God, we believe you call us to love each other as we do ourselves,
God, with all our hearts, we will strive to love our brothers and sisters from every denomination and group.
God, we believe you ask us to use our gifts to serve each other in unity and understanding,
God, may we, in a spirit of love and care, use our gifts to build each other up.
God, we believe that in unity together we will come to a full knowledge of Christ,
God, may we grow together into the knowledge of the one in whom all things fit together.

Our Father who is in heaven hallowed be your name. Your kingdom come, your will be done, on earth as it is in heaven. Give us this day our daily bread and forgive us our trespasses as we forgive those who trespass against us. Lead us not into temptation but deliver us from evil, for yours is the kingdom the power and the glory, forever and ever. Amen.

God, we believe you have called us to unity, but often we have isolated ourselves from others,
God, forgive us for the times we have turned our backs on those who are different.
God, we believe you have called us to live together as one body,
God, forgive us for the times we have created division within your worldwide community.
God, we believe you ask us to look, listen, and learn from others,
God, forgive us for the times we have ridiculed and attacked those with different viewpoints.
God, we believe you ask us to accept and seek to understand all who are called by your name,
Forgive us for the times we have offended you by failing to love others as we do ourselves.
God, we believe you call us to be one even as you are one,
Forgive us for the disunity we have harbored and make us one.

Pause to offer up prayers for unity within the church.

God and Creator of all humankind, your son Jesus Christ prayed that your church might be one even as you our God are one. May you renew our minds and rekindle your love in our hearts, so that by the power of the Spirit, we might find the Oneness that you intend for us.

God, may we see in your Oneness our need for unity,
God, may we see in your Three-ness our need for community
God, may we see in your creativity our need for diversity,
God, may we see in your Self our need to love each other.
Amen.

MONDAY

"The Reality of Diversity"
Eliacín Rosario-Cruz

"What do you mean by 'just one'? I'm not choosing just one!" I told my wife on the phone. She had told me that according to the educational department of our city, in order to register our daughter in an educational program, I needed to choose just one box to indicate my ethnicity.

The options given to me were:

___Latino/Hispanic of:
___A. Black ancestry
___B. White ancestry
___C. Indigenous ancestry

Taken into consideration that, as a Puerto Rican, I was born into the mestizo-rich heritage of Taino indigenous people, White Europeans mostly from Spain, and Black Africans brought to my country as slaves, to mark only one box would be to reject two of the key heritages that make me who I am. To allow myself to be boxed into one would be to reject many members of my family and many aspects of my culture and identity that I am proud of. I would therefore cease to be me. I am not me by just one part of my ancestry, but by the gifts I accept from all three of them.

This was, to say the least, an extremely uncomfortable situation for me. I was forced by a detached system to make a choice I never thought of making. I was irate because of the way in which this systemic, violent act of identity distortion goes unnoticed daily by the super-structures in a society that won't tolerate and in fact discourages the embracing of multiple identities.

Normal everyday activities like going to the doctor's office, playing at the park, and registering your child for an art class shouldn't make you question your identity and wonder if there are other people out there like you. At some level, I can expect the State and the framework that supports its philosophies to try to fit everyone into one box. After all, people are easier to manage and be marketed when they belong to a generic group with already-given narratives and attributes.

I have the greater trouble with the system when it comes to matters of spirituality. What if, to that list of activities/places/institutions that make us question our place, we add places of worship, communities of faith, and new expressions of Christianity? How are we to respond to the worldwide community of God's children when our way of coming together at the Lord's Table for prayer, discipleship, and service not only reflects, but also perpetuates divisiveness, discrimination, and oppression?

Not many of us can stay away from confronting our dark side. We avoid the pain it causes to be naked and vulnerable, especially when it is something we have the privilege to not experience. While many live in constant vulnerability due to their color, place of origin, language, sexual orientation, gender, or class, others enjoy the benefit of going through life with little to no experience of what is to be on the underside of power, oppression, and control and in the margins. Our communities of faith and places of worship are called to be places of healing and restitution. But they do not exist in a vacuum. Our churches and places of worship are not only part of our societies, but they are formed by individuals and groups with certain stories, myths, and patterns. These constructs surround and give a framework for our actions and our relationship with others. When these unarticulated beliefs and values go unexamined and unquestioned, we run the risk of living sub-human lives.

If communities of faith are to be a real place of radical hospitality and transformative relationships, they need to deal with the social constructs in which they inhabit. The social expression of the church and individual Christians does not happen outside the artificial modes of thinking about the actuality of power and privilege. We will do more damage than good if we keep addressing the issues of faith and social justice without questioning the given frameworks of racism, patriarchy, hetero/sexism, classism, and elitism. It is by pushing farther past the strings and paradigms by which the church functions that we as followers of Jesus can honestly bring a healing alternative and prophetic voice. It is by rendering visible these chains of affliction that we can move from hollow cosmetic corrections and into real salvation and transformation. Given that we are blind to our own complicity and that we have the tendency to describe things to our advantage, we need the voice of "the other" for a broader expression of God's goodness and liberation.

This is not easy work. It involves the painful act of carrying our own cross, but also helping others carry theirs. The movement toward humanization confronts us with the scandal that those who have been marginalized bring to our realities. As we move further into this journey of examination and confrontation, we allow space for the creation of new intersections for mutual understanding, transformation, and affirmation. It is at this point that we are less worried about the scandal that others bring, and are more open to fully experience the gifts we receive from them. It is at this moment that we begin to live in the reality of the Risen Christ.

✛

Eliacín Rosario-Cruz is originally from sunny Puerto Rico, making his home now the in cloudy Pacific Northwest. He loves coffee, reading and grilling. He tries not to give in to the temptation of sounding too important while weirdly writing this bio in third person.

TUESDAY

"Thirsting for Justice in a Society of Growing Inequity"
Tom Sine

I had the wonderful opportunity, from 1977 to 1984 to head a community development project in Haiti for World Concern. We were invited by village leaders in the Pleasant Valley to work with them to improve the quality of life of 10,000 people who lived in this community. People were barely subsisting on an annual income of $150 a person a year. Children were frequently dying of malnutrition. 60% of the illnesses came from drinking polluted water from streams they shared with their cattle.

We worked with these leaders to drill wells for safe water, increase food production and create a village level healthcare system. However, the village leaders told us that there top priority was to construct a road so that they could safely get their products to market in other villages.

They also told us that one of the major reasons constructing the road was their top priority was that they wanted "justice to come down the road." It wasn't until months later that we finally learned what this meant. In their community like communities all over the world the powerful and wealthy too often taken advantage of the poor. We learned in this community a few wealthy land owners were routinely taking away land from poor farmers under the guise of changes in the law.

Since these poor farmers had no way to contest having their land stolen they wanted "justice to come down the road." They wanted to construct a road so that leaders from the national government could come in reverse this misappropriation of their land.

My Australian Christian friends ask a great question:" what is God on about?" In other words what are God's purposes for a people and a world? Too many Christians believe God's purposes focus almost exclusively on private faith and personal pursuit of righteousness. Too often they don't recognize that God's purposes include societal change too. bringing healing to the broken, justice to the poor and peace to the nations as well.

In response to the growing inequity that characterized society in Israel, God called on the people to institute "Jubilee." This economic structural change was intended to end generational poverty and give every family a fresh start every 50 years. Not surprisingly those in power resisted this call to justice and jubilee was not widely practiced.

But Isaiah, Jeremiah, Micah and the other prophets all spoke truth to power, often at the risk of their own lives. They not only called individuals to live more righteously; they also called the whole society to operate more justly.

As we journey with Jesus towards Jerusalem there is greater inequity in America than any other developed country. Regrettably that inequity is growing. *The New York Times* reported on March 21 that between 1993 to 2010 incomes of the richest 1% of Americans grew 58% while the rest of us only experienced a 6.4% gain.

In the important book *Nickel and Dimed*,[45] the author describes in vivid terms how many of those who serve us in restaurants and hotels barely subsist on their low incomes. A surprising number live in their cars and housing that is unsafe. What's new since the recession is that growing numbers of the middle class are beginning to struggle to just subsist like the working poor have done for years.

Isn't it time for followers of Jesus to speak truth to power? Shouldn't we be calling our communities, corporations and government to increase educational and employment opportunities for all people to prosper and enjoy the fruit of their labor.... not just those for this new class of the super rich?

There is a new philosophy of extreme individualism that is becoming popular America. This philosophy does not find its roots in Scripture but rather as a product of the Enlightenment. In its simplest form it asserts that if we all pursue our own self-interest it will automatically work for the common good. The reality is that too often when people of power wealth and privilege pursue their own self-interest, it centralizes wealth and power for the few at the expense of many of the rest of us.... like we saw in Haiti.

Listen in this season of Lent. Listen to the call of the prophet Isaiah to participate in a fast that hungers and thirsts for justice. Particularly note how this passage contradicts the ideology of individual pursuit of self-interest. It makes clear that our healing and well-being is directly connected to the well-being of our neighbors.

Isaiah asks if God calls us to a fast where we simply humble ourselves:

"Is that what you call a fast, a day acceptable to the Lord? Is not this the kind of fasting I have chosen: to loose the chains of injustice and untie the cords of the yoke, to set the oppressed free and break every yoke? Is it not to share your food with the hungry and to provide the poor wanderer with shelter–when you see the naked clothe him, and not to turn away from your own flesh and blood?'

Then your light will break forth like the dawn and your healing will quickly appear; then your righteousness will go before you and the glory of the Lord will be your rear guard. Then you will call, and the Lord will answer, you will cry for help, and he will say: Here am I. If you do away with the yoke of oppression with the pointing finger and the malicious talk, and if you spend yourselves in behalf the hungry and satisfy the needs of the oppressed, then your life will rise in the darkness and your night will become like noonday" (Isaiah 58: 6-10, NIV).

Tom Sine is a consultant in futures research and planning for both Christian and secular organizations. He has a wonderful gift of hospitality and loves cooking for friends. His most recent book is The New Conspirators: Creating the Future One Mustard Seed At A Time. *More information about Tom and his work can be found at* <u>msaimagine.org</u>.

Wednesday

"Identity, Intimacy & Impact"
AnaYelsi Sanchez

Intimacy with God enables us to maintain a passion for justice and a commitment to living in solidarity with our brothers and sisters in poverty. Intimacy with God opens up the door to intimacy with others.

But what is intimacy? Is it emotional? Spiritual? Sexual? Experiential?

And is intimacy taught or is it simply a part of what It is to be human?

Many of us share this passion for justice, though it may not always look the same. If you were to ask my friends and colleagues what I have a great passion for, what lights a fire in my spirit, makes me sit up straighter, and speak a little louder, they would tell you- Human Trafficking.

For others it may be a desire to see equality for the LGBT community, another might seek to improve the quality of life for the Sudanese refugees living here in Omaha, and so on and so forth.

No matter what the cause, our ability to impact issues of injustice is directly connected to our ability to experience healthy intimacy and our ability to experience healthy intimacy is directly connected to our sense of identity.

How do we tell a woman trapped in Kolkata's sex trafficking industry that she is valuable and beautiful if we do not believe this about ourselves?

How do we encourage a child living on the streets of Peru that God AND others want to know them and want to share a life with them when we don't know the depths of that type of relationship ourselves?

Hear me when I say that this is not about perfecting self before you can serve others.

Identity, Intimacy, Impact... this is a continuous cycle... not a hierarchy of achievements.

If you have an incredible sense of self-worth and identity but never look beyond yourself than you have missed the point. And if you are celebrated for your acts of service and your fervor for justice but cannot even be vulnerable about who you are with those who love you, than you have cheated yourself. God is a God of intimacy AND of action. She desires for us to know her, each other, AND ourselves…. and then to use that knowledge to bring about peace and justice.

But, most of us do not even know what it is to be intimate with our self and yet, how we relate to the world is a reflection of how we relate to our self. When you consider that, it is easy to understand why we are rarely truly intimate with others.

How often are you alone with yourself? How often do you spend time studying who you are and working on your sense of self?

Born in Caracas, Venezuela, AnaYelsi Sanchez came to the U.S as a toddler and has lived a life that has provided firsthand insight into issues of economic inequality, sexism, and racism. As well as being an artist, AnaYelsi is a passionate women and LGBT rights advocate. She is also a dedicated and trained anti-slavery activist. These passions often seep into her creative endeavors - resulting in art that strives to push people beyond observation into engagement. The desire is to challenge the observer to change a world that is too often steeped in injustice, imbalances, and harsh realities.

THURSDAY

"Glocal Christianity"
Matt Stone

A few years ago, I named my blog "Glocal Christianity." Here is a reflection of why I chose that name. I am sure many of you wonder what the heck I mean by 'glocal' and what that has to do with my style of Christianity, so here goes.

Glocalization
The word 'glocalization' is a portmanteau of the words 'glocal' and 'local'. It's basically short for 'localized globalization', and unpacks the fact that the globalization of the local (macro-localization) and the localization of the global (micro-globalization) are often intertwined.

To give some examples, who doesn't know what a vuvuzela is now? The infliction of vuvuzela's on the world by South African soccer fans is a classic example of macro-localization, of the universalization of the particular. Conversely, who's heard of the expression, "The world is at your doorstep?" The existence of 45 language groups in a school near me in western Sydney is a classic example of micro-globalization, of the particularization of the universal. These are some of the experiences and truths I seek to grapple with in this blog.

Some locales are more globalized than others
Now, the truth of the matter is that some locales are more globalized than others. By and large, towns are not as glocalized as cities, small cities are not as glocalized as large cities, and even within large cities some suburbs are not as glocalized as others. Of course there are exceptions, but that's the general rule of thumb.

My interest is born of the fact that I just happen to live in one of the most multicultural suburbs in one of the most multicultural cities in the Southern Hemisphere. Glocalization is rampant. So I wonder, what does a glocalized Christianity look like?

What does glocalized Christianity look like?
First, I tell you what it doesn't look like, at least for me. It doesn't look like Celtic revivalist Christianity, for Celtic nostalgia is only one influence amongst many. It doesn't look like triumphalist civic Christianity, for Christianity is becoming

increasingly marginalized in this religious milieu. It doesn't look like a menagerie of neotribal Christianities, for we've got far more subcultures than Christians. It doesn't look like emerging expressions of Christianity in less globalized locales. It has far more diversity to grapple with.

So, what will a glocalized Christianity look like? That's what I've been exploring and what I hope to explore in even greater depth as my own understanding expands. As I have expressed in my blog description, at the very least I think it involves exploring what it means to follow Jesus in a multireligious, multicultural, multimedia world. And I differentiate between multireligious and multicultural quite deliberately. I think it's equally important to explore how we disciple western Hindus and eastern Christians. In fact, I am continually challenged to do both without walking more than 20 meters from my front door. A glocalized Christianity is a Christianity adapted for contexts of extreme cultural and religious diversity. That's what this is about, both the conversations and the art.

The web as globalized locale

Now, of course extreme cultural and religious diversity may not be your local experience. Diversity is distributed unevenly and by virtue of that we are each going to have different experiences. But, I'm gathering if you spend much time on the Internet that you've experienced at least some of the ripple effects of glocalization. And I'm gathering you probably recognize that the web itself is a globalized locale, albeit a nonphysical one. I'm glad we can join on this journey of discovery, of exploring what it looks like to follow Jesus in a multireligious, multicultural, multimedia world.

Matt Stone is a blogger from Sydney, Australia, and has been blogging about world religions since 2004. His writing flows out of experiences amongst Christians, Hindus, Buddhists, Wiccans and the "spiritual but not religious," both as a Christian and prior to that. His work may be found at mattstone.blogs.com.

FRIDAY

"Hiroshima"
James Rempt

God's family is in no way exempt from experiencing the brokenness of this struggling world, and yet more than once I have learned that God's life giving hands of healing in renewal can be seen in even the most despairing places. Learning to recognize this is an important step in anyone's faith journey. Undoubtedly, the degree to which this brokenness causes us to be estranged from our neighbor becomes increasingly evident as we reach beyond and through the complicated barriers made fast by history, political confrontation, the tensions of frictional faith traditions and the rifts caused by cultural differences. However, as we continue to journey past these barriers, the dysfunction of our world may also be challenged, and God's work towards the reunification of His family may be witnessed in powerful ways.

In my life, perhaps, one of the most notable instances of being surprised by a glimmer of hope in an unlikely place occurred when I pushed through the barriers of culture and history and stepped into the brokenness of Hiroshima, Japan.

It was August 2008, and the heat of southern Japan was sweltering. Nearly 100 degrees with close to 90% humidity, I felt as if I might melt as my two traveling companions and I walked into a small church in Hiroshima. A hospitable pastor had agreed to let each of us sleep on a church pew for about 9 dollars a night. As we unloaded our baggage in a room beside the sanctuary, we found relief. We were visiting Hiroshima to participate in the atomic bomb memorial ceremonies, commemorating the tragedy that occurred some 63 years previous.

The dynamics associated with our travel alone represented the notable weight of history and cultural tension. The three of us had met several years previous while studying in Canada. While we all shared the same faith, our nationalities spanned three different countries: America, Japan, and China. It had already been a remarkable aspect of our travels in Japan, going through historic sites related to World War II, and listening to my Chinese friend quietly notify us that the statistics and history we read on signs and placards were in fact wrong, according to the history he had learned in China. Japan, as he underscored with restrained surprise and a touch of irony in his voice, had killed many more civilians in

China, and committed much more grievous atrocities than the museums there reported.

That evening, our host invited us to join him and one of his coworkers for okonomiyaki, a type of savory pancake that has become quite famous, especially in southern Japan. The food was satisfying, and my Japanese travel companion, fluent in both English and Japanese, made it possible for all of us to enjoy lively conversation. At the end of our meal, I offered to cover the bill. The pastor hesitated momentarily and then said something quickly to my Japanese friend. She translated for me, "In Japan, we never let our Japanese guests pay for meals even when they offer, because we know they are just being polite. But you are an American, so we know you mean what you say." I paid, we received directions for visiting certain portions of the city, and with the remaining daylight we departed to investigate the left over historical ruins specifically preserved as a reminder of the destruction of the atomic bomb.

The next morning we left the church before eight in order to get a seat in the outdoor park where thousands congregated to hear the addresses of diplomats and politicians from around the world. With the aid of ear pieces wired directly to real time translations of the speeches, we were able to discern that the event was as much about a memorial to the destruction of the city as it was about a deep commitment to peace. But something else continued to grab my attention in the midst of the oppressive heat. Somewhere out of site on the outskirts of the park, we heard people yelling. I asked my Japanese friend what they were saying, but she wasn't sure, only that they were protesting something.

I counted only five other white faces in Hiroshima that day. In retrospect, I feel as if this should have been a source of discomfort for me, especially at an event mourning acts of war committed by my country. But the Japanese people there were not aggressive or even angry: instead there was a mournful sorrow lingering in the air, and an even more notable dynamic of desired hope for the future (this was a stark contrast from the "peace museums" of Vietnam I would visit several years later).

While the museums chalked full of ghastly photographs, burned out skeletons of buildings purposely left standing as a reminder of the raw destruction of the bomb, and the shadows eerily resembling human forms burned into the pavement have been etched in my memory, two things in particular stood out in my mind from our experience of the city that day, August 6, 2008.

First, we learned a survivor of the atomic bomb would be sharing her story at the World Friendship Center, just blocks away from the hypocenter of the atomic bomb. The three of us unanimously agreed to attend her sharing time there, and it was one of the more humbling and impactful moments of my life.

I learned while in Hiroshima that survivors of the bomb, called "hibakusha", were largely shunned. Given the high number of injuries, the early deaths, lingering health issues and resultant birth defects associated with those who had been near the atomic bombings in Japan, they were stigmatized, often deemed unmarriageable and forced to hide their cities of origin. All this AFTER being fortunate enough to survive one of the single most destructive acts in modern history.

As we entered the World Friendship Center, a Quaker affiliated facility dedicated to serving the people of Hiroshima and supporting various global peace initiatives, I was surprised by how small it was. Nearly at capacity with less than 25 visitors (mostly from Australia and New Zealand), we were among the last to arrive. We sat down on the floor just before an elderly Japanese woman with one eye sat down in a chair in the front of the room.

"I was at work in a factory," she said. "Even though I was only a teenager, because of the war, many of those who would otherwise have been studying had to work." She went on to recollect the sound of the air raid sirens leading up to the explosion. A portion of the ceiling collapsed as the bomb detonated, and struck her in the eye.

As she continued to share how the effects of the bomb impacted her life, the family she loved and her community, I was greatly humbled as an American. Just days before, I didn't even know the term "hibakusha", let alone that an entire community of survivors had experienced nothing less than persecution simply for being near or from a city affected by the atomic bomb. This was brokenness, and it was tied not only to the history of my nation but also my own family history. My grandfather had also lost the use of his eye during WWII, only his injury occurred while fighting the Japanese in the Pacific.

After the time of sharing, we were invited for lunch. I was seated next to the sweet elderly woman who had suffered so much as a result of the bombing. Even my immediate family has rarely met the depths of sharing that her story of suffering and shame encountered. We ate together, and with the help of a translator shared not just food, but real conversation. I will never forget that meal, and I will never forget the grace of the woman who had so much taken from her as a result of my own nation's political interests.

The second lesson that impacted me that day happened later in the same day. When we returned that night, exhausted emotionally and physically, we learned that we would not be alone in the church. A small group of college students had arrived to stay as well. As we made ready for bed in the small space, I attempted to speak with them. They quieted, and I quickly learned that while they all wanted to communicate, due to varying English proficiencies, only a couple of them could speak English with confidence. Fortunately, my Japanese friend translated.

As we attempted to draw one another out, I asked them if they had heard the protestors near the park that day. They nodded in affirmation, looking shy. "You see," one explained, "we were the protestors." My eyes widened, and I immediately tried to welcome this piece of news by looking impressed and asking them what they were protesting. "We were protesting nuclear energy in Japan." Immediately, we dove into a conversation regarding the history of nuclear activity in Japan. I explained to them how I regretted the way my nation justified the use of the bomb in their country, and I attempted to explain that the United States was likely serving a complicated group of interests, far beyond a utilitarian and final end to the Pacific war. "After all, it wasn't just that America was at war," I told them, "America needed to show the Russians what we had, in order to balance military power in favor of the U.S."

Sitting in this church, the students went on to share their concern regarding nuclear energy production in Japan. This conversation seems prophetic in hindsight, considering the meltdown of the Fukushima reactor less than three years later, the fall out of which is still poisoning the surrounding area with harmful amounts of radiation.

As we neared the end of our conversation, one girl who had quietly folded a piece of paper throughout the whole discussion handed me a beautiful piece of origami and smiled.

Slowly, all of us gave in to exhaustion, eventually picking different church pews and finally nodding off to sleep in our sleeping bags.

A lot was happening in that church, to be sure. Barriers were transcended. Those barriers could have just as easily been reinforced. The weight of the place in itself was immense, as were the events commemorated and the circumstances protested that day. Yet these barriers were overcome. I shared trusted space with those who only moments before had been unknown, faceless protestors and voices of opposition. Those who were strangers became neighbors in that church, all of us on a journey to the same place, the Hiroshima memorial, a place of brokenness, the site of one of the single most serious and destructive acts of warfare in all history. We found shelter together and connected amidst diversity, in spite of our differences. In that church, there was dialogue where before there had been none. And there was unexpected joy in this for me: It was the joy of discovery, the joy of being known, the exploration of perspective, and the joy of connection between those of faith and those who professed none. The tension at work there made our sharing time all the more beautiful. Later, my Japanese friend would tell me that never in her life had she heard other Japanese people share about these matters in such a way.

A great deal came together in Hiroshima. A journey into brokenness was a step towards growth, restoration, and I believe the healing of my understanding (if not others). It was all the more wonderful that it took place amidst the history and the brokenness of that city. My experience in Hiroshima served to broaden not only my understanding of what happens in a church, but also how God's family is shaped, how God's family interacts with brokenness, and how God's family experiences healing. It is my hope that circumstances such as these will carry on into the future and the restoration of not only Hiroshima, but the entirety of God's family as we journey past the barriers.

A graduate of Trinity Western University, James Rempt currently works as a contractor for an investment firm in Seattle, where he also lives. He enjoys hiking, writing, fishing, playing music and working cross culturally, and is currently supporting a small church plant in the Seattle area.

SATURDAY

"Pointing at the Moon"
Monette Chilson

When faced with belief systems different from ours, we can focus on the similarities or see only the differences. The choice is ours, and the results can be profound. Division or unity. Argument or conversation. In our propensity to stake a claim for the legitimacy of our faith, we can over-focus on distinctions that set "us" apart from "them."

I remember a rush of relief—a sense that God was at work in grander ways than exacting theologians ever suspected—when I discovered that the guiding principles of yoga (yama and niyama) were exactly the same as the Ten Commandments which, of course, were already the bedrock of the Jewish faith. And that this same moral compass was imbedded into the Qur'an and woven into Buddha's Eight Fold Path.

Seeing these points of convergence among religions can be extremely comforting. The similarities point to something bigger and more powerful than any one religion can encapsulate within its boundaries. These synchronicities— these moments where tongues that speak different languages and find their sacred words in different books are all singing the same song—remind me that God is so much more than even the most sacred of scriptures can put into words. God cannot be contained within a system devised by humans.

This is one of the truths we could experience if we all belonged to a club like the one Rayna Idliby, Suzanne Oliver, and Priscilla Warner chronicled in their book *The Faith Club: A Muslim, A Christian, a Jew—Three Women Searching for Understanding.*[46]

Dr. William F. Vendley, Secretary General for the World Conference of Religions for Peace, recommends the book, saying,

> Three contemporary women...search together across divides of prejudice and fear. Their honesty becomes a path to connection; their courage leads into the ranges of the heart opened by their own religions. Working together, they each arrive where alone they could not go.[47]

He is not describing a high-level religious summit organized by an international coalition to promote interfaith relations. This is just three moms sitting down and getting honest about their faiths, their backgrounds, and their fears. These are [people] just like us. What if people across the country started forming their own faith clubs? What if we intentionally sought out those with different beliefs, forged relationships, and engaged in authentic dialog while traversing the terrain of our differences, with the goal of arriving in a space where we can co-exist?

I am reminded of a Sufi tale used by Joan Chittister in her book *Called to Question*. She relays the story of Sufi disciples who, at their spiritual master's death bed, mourned his imminent departure, pleading, "If you leave us, Master, how will we know what to do?" In the beautiful, mystical way of the Sufis, the master replied, "I am nothing but a finger pointing at the moon. Perhaps when I am gone, you will see the moon."[48]

When I gaze at the moon, I find great joy in the knowledge that so many others are soaking up that same beauty. Will you join me tonight? Together, let's see if it's possible to appreciating the fullness of the moon's luminous beauty without having to own it or claim it as our own.

Monette Chilson has practiced yoga for two decades and is dedicated to demystifying the spiritual benefits of yoga. Her work has appeared in Yoga Journal, Integral Yoga Magazine, Om Times *and* Christian Yoga Magazine, *and her first book,* Sophia Rising: Awakening Your Sacred Wisdom Through Yoga, *was released by Bright Sky Press in June 2013. Read more at www.SophiaRisingYoga.com. This contributeion was reprinted by permission of Bright Sky Press.*

HOLY WEEK AND EASTER:

JOURNEY FROM PALM SUNDAY TO THE CROSS

ENTER THE JOURNEY

> "Anything is possible in a world in which a Jewish carpenter can rise from the dead."[49]

Holy week, the final week of Lent, commemorates the events of Christ's last week before his death. For many of Christ's followers, it was a roller coaster ride, beginning with his triumphal entry into Jerusalem and ending with his death on the cross.

Holy week begins Palm Sunday with Jesus entering Jerusalem as the Messiah promised long ago by God. An enthusiastic crowd spread palm branches along the road as a symbol of triumph and victory, shouting "Hosanna to the Son of David! Blessed is he who comes in the name of the Lord! Hosanna in the highest!"[50] All of Jerusalem must have buzzed with the news of his coming. Jew and Gentile alike were caught up in the contagion, rejoicing with enthusiasm at the man passing on the donkey.

Your Palm Sunday meeting is the last Lenten get together with your group. Begin by looking back over the last week. What new insights have you gained into the nature of God and God's family? What long-term changes have they encouraged you to make?

Now look ahead. What are some ways that you might in the future be able to include people from your neighborhood, or even from across the world, in this celebration of the Good News of Christ over Holy Week or the Easter weekend?

Here are some suggestions:

- If you walk around your neighborhood for your Palm Sunday procession, consider knocking on doors around your church and inviting people to a Palm Sunday potluck celebration at the church.
- If your church is a little more adventurous, you may like to plan a larger celebration and invite people several weeks in advance. Get permission to cordon off the road in front of the church and plan a BBQ or meet in the local park. Then on Palm Sunday do a procession through the neighborhood and invite people again to make sure that they know they are included. Don't neglect the marginalized people in your community. Make a point of visiting the local homeless shelter, or visit the local senior care facility and bring out the people in wheelchairs for the feast.

As the last act of our journey, we invite you to join us in reliving this final week of Christ's life.

Read through the gospel account of Jesus' journey from the time of his entry into Jerusalem until he is laid in the tomb (John 18:1 – 19:42).

- Which event most catches your attention? Reread this part of the story several times aloud.
- Imagine yourself walking beside Jesus at this point of his journey. What aspect of your own life comes to mind as you read?
- Spend time in silence reflecting on the Scripture.
- Now get creative. Write a poem, reflection, or prayer, draw a picture, make a sculpture out of wood, clay, or paper, or take a photo that captures the essence of this part of the story for you.
- Send your offerings to us at mail@msaimagine.org. Make sure that you let us know which part of the story they apply to.
- We will publish these on the Godspace blog on Good Friday.

A Litany for Good Friday

Jesus Christ, Savior of our world,
Redeemer of all creation,
The bringer of health and wholeness,
We bless and praise your name.
You died for us and hung upon a cross,
Your blood was shed and your body broken,
So that we might be set free,
We bless and praise your name.

*Pause to reflect on the cross and the ways you have been transformed because of Christ's
sacrifice.*

Have mercy on us,
Son of the living God,
Healer of lepers, feeder of the hungry,
Releaser of the oppressed, bringer of wholeness,
Christ crucified, Eternal God
Have mercy on us.

Help us to lay down our own lives daily,
And consciously take on Christ's life,
**May we consider the needs of others as more important than our
own,**
Teach us, Lord, to live the life of the cross.
Enable us to live a life of service and not of selfish ambition,
Empower us to reach out with compassion and care,
May we identify with the poor, the marginalized, and the vulnerable,
Teach us, Lord, to live the life of the cross.
Encourage us to extend ourselves in serving and loving,
Being willing to walk the extra mile,
May we reach out to all those who suffer and are in pain.
Teach us, Lord, to live the life of the cross.
Forgive us for when we discard Christ's life,
And so quickly reach for our own ways again,
**For it is in dying to ourselves that we find life and enter the ways of
your kingdom.**
Teach us, Lord, to live the life of the cross.

Read Scripture passages for the day from your chosen resource.

God, we believe you sent your Son to redeem us,
Jesus Christ showed us the path from death to life.
He led us to the cross, where sin dies and freedom flows,
Where despair is transformed into hope,
Where pain and healing embrace.
God, we believe the cross is the ultimate outpouring of God's love for all humankind.
At the cross we are saved from our sins,
Our suffering gives birth to joy,
Our brokenness is transformed into wholeness.
Our death is resurrected into new life.
We believe you ask us to lay down our lives at the foot of the cross,
At the cross we repent of our self-centered ways,
And acknowledge daily your incarnate presence within us.
We believe we must journey with you through the agony of crucifixion,
To find true life as we give it away.
We must move through the horror of death to the joy of resurrection
and new life.

Our Father in heaven, hallowed be your name. Your Kingdom come, your will be done, on earth as in heaven. Give us today our daily bread. Forgive us our sins, as we forgive those who sin against us. Lead us not into temptation, but deliver us from evil. For the kingdom, the power and the glory are yours. Now and forever. Amen

Father God, today we lay our burdens at the foot of the cross,
Burdens we have shouldered that you did not intend for us.
Lord, forgive us for the pain we have given you.
We have taken lightly the sacrifice of your son,
And have turned our backs on your redemptive love,
Lord, forgive us for ways in which we have ignored your salvation.
We have become bound up in our own fears and anxieties,
We have doubted your caring concern for all our needs.
Lord, forgive us for denying your faithfulness to provide day by day.
We have fretted over seeds we have planted that have not yet begun to grow,
And forgotten that you are the one who brings growth and provides fruit.
Lord, forgive us for disregarding your generous guidance in all we do.

We strive in our independence to accomplish alone tasks you mean us to share,
And so deny the concern and support of a God who speaks through community.
Lord, forgive us for our selfish love and self-centered living.
We have abandoned the poor, the destitute and the marginalized,
And so denied your love and compassion for all who are made in your image.
Lord, forgive us for failing to see your divine image reflected in friends and strangers.

God, we want to kneel at the foot of your cross and listen,
Open our eyes that we might be aware of your faithfulness,
Open our ears that we might hear your instruction,
Open our arms that we might share your generosity,
Open our hearts that we might be embraced by your love.

God, we have invited you into the dark and hidden places of our lives,
We have chosen the way of the cross,
You have washed away our sins and cleansed us with your blood.
Be with us this day in crucifixion and resurrection,
So that the light of Christ can truly shine out through every part of us,
Amen.

Palm Sunday

"Palm Sunday is Coming, But What Does it Mean?"
Christine Sine

Today is Palm Sunday and many of our churches are busy making palm frond crosses or preparing for a walk around our churches as a start to the day. Most of us know that this day commemorates Jesus triumphant procession into Jerusalem on donkey's back but few of us are aware of the deeper implications of this event. Jesus triumphal entry into Jerusalem may have begun with crowds shouting "Hosanna!" but it ends with Good Friday and the apparent triumph of the powers of the Roman Empire and of Satan. It does not end with a gold crown but with a crown of thorns. Jesus triumphal entry ends with his willingness to take into himself all the pain and suffering of our world so that together we can celebrate the beginning of a new procession on Easter Sunday – a procession that leads us into God's banquet feast and the wonder of God's eternal world.

Over the last couple of years I have written several blog posts that talk about the subversive nature of this event. I have reread these this morning and realized how much I needed this reminder. So I thought that I would adapt them here for all of us to remember once again and meditate on the meaning of this event.

The beginning of the Easter celebration is just over a week away and stores are full of Easter eggs and decorations to help us celebrate by diverting our attention from the real meaning of Easter to their commercialized version of it. And how many of us are sucked in? What is the focus of your celebrations for this Holy week – is it on the life, death and resurrection of Christ or is it on the upcoming Easter egg hunt and that new spring outfit that you intend to debut on Easter Sunday morning?

Our Easter celebration should begin with Palm Sunday a celebration in which we excitedly enter into a preview of Jesus announcing his Messiahship and the advent of God's kingdom of wholeness and abundance. What many of us don't realize is that there were actually two processions into Jerusalem on that Palm Sunday morning – one that symbolized the Roman culture of Jesus' day and the other Jesus proclaiming his upside-down kingdom.

In the year 30, Pontius Pilate was the Roman governor assigned to Judea and Jerusalem. It had become the custom of the governors to live outside Jerusalem, but it was also their custom to come with their soldiers to Jerusalem for Passover. To provide a very visible and powerful Roman military presence at that volatile time, to prevent any potential uprising, for there are already been uprisings and many crucifixions.

His procession would have come from the west at the head of a column of imperial cavalry and soldiers – an impressive and lavish procession specially designed to impress the people with a visual display of imperial power: cavalry on horses, foot soldiers, leather armor, helmets, weapons, banners, golden eagles mounted on poles, sun glinting on metal and gold.

On the other side of the city, down from the Mount of Olives in the north came Jesus and his humble procession – no pomp, no ceremony, dressed simply like the people, riding on the back of a donkey and followed by his disciples drawn from amongst the peasants and the common people. I can imagine the lepers he had healed and the once blind man dancing and rejoicing with him. And there is Lazarus with Mary and Martha, a living symbol of the triumph that this procession represents.

Here was the truly triumphant procession and the true rejoicing of the season. Jesus and his friends were greeted with cheers and shouts by crowds all along his path. "Hosanna! Blessed is the one who comes in the name of the Lord! Hosanna!"[51]

Much of what Jesus' life and teaching was about was the conflict of the kingdom of God with the empire of Rome: theologically and politically. The Romans believed their emperor was to be worshipped as the son of God, the savior of humankind.

When Jesus rode into Jerusalem and his followers acknowledged him as Lord and Messiah, this was not only a personal theological statement but a political statement as well. Jesus' belief in a liberating, inclusive, non-violent, peace-seeking kingdom of God was over and against the oppressive, greedy, elite-loving, peasant-starving kingdom of Rome. No wonder his was so angry with the Temple hierarchy – the chief priest, the elders and the scribes – who had become servants of the empire and not of the kingdom of God.

Jesus' ride into Jerusalem was obviously headed for a collision with the powerful Roman empire—collision that would cost his life and change history forever.

The question for all of us as we approach this Palm Sunday and enter into the celebration of Easter is: Where is our allegiance? Where do we find ourselves in these pictures? Are we part of that ragamuffin discipleship band following Jesus fully aware that we are on a collision course with the values of our secular culture? Are we some of the misguided enthusiasts, cheering our own idea of a messiah, that looks more like the Roman emperor than the humble Jesus? Are we enamored of an idea that has little to do with what Jesus has come to teach? Do we only want to follow a Jesus when we think he promises health and happiness here and now. Have we so misunderstood him and his purpose and that we are ready to turn against him when he turns out not to be who we thought he was?

Perhaps however, we're not part of Jesus' procession at all. Perhaps we're standing at the other gate, cheering for the symbols of empire. Dazzled by power, attracted to wealth, wanting to identify with the victors, not the vanquished, hoping to be counted as one of the elites of our time.

Actually most of us are probably part of both processions – wanting to follow this Jesus whom we find we don't fully understand but also caught up in the excitement of Easter egg hunts and spring fashion displays.

And the beauty is that Jesus, in his humanity, sees and knows all of us. . . the flawed humanity that surrounds him. . . the flawed humanity of each of us. . . He sees it and he forgives it, he loves us, and gives his blessing to all of us as he clops along the dusty road toward his confrontation with power, his time of trial, his abandonment, his death.

Christine Sine is the Executive Director of Mustard Seed Associates. She trained as a physician in Australia and developed the medical ministry for Mercy Ships. She now speaks on issues relating to changing our timestyles and lifestyles to develop a more spiritual rhythm for life. She has authored several books including Return to Our Senses: Reimagining How We Pray; Godspace: Time for Peace in the Rhythms of Life; *and* Tales of a Seasick Doctor. *Christine blogs at http://godspace-msa.com.*

MONDAY

"The Good Samaritan: A Re-Boot"
David Backes

The idea of placing Jesus into a modern setting and putting a classic parable into modern context has been in my head for a while, but this is the first time I've tried it. Here goes:

Jesus was in Washington, D.C., speaking at the annual National Prayer Breakfast. A politician well-known for strong religious views stood up to test him and said, "Jesus, what must I do to inherit eternal life?"

Jesus responded, "What is written in God's law? How do you understand it?"

The politician said, "You shall love God with all your heart, all your being, all your strength and all your mind, and your neighbor as yourself." Jesus replied, "You said it well. Do this and you will live."

Looking for a loophole, the politician pressed Jesus: "And how would you define 'neighbor'?"

Jesus answered with a story. "A poor nation on a remote continent suffered a devastating drought; hundreds of thousands were dying of thirst and famine, and then disease broke out and the death toll continued to climb. The whole world watched with horror as newscasts showed the immensity of the suffering.

"Many of the people who watched lived in wealthy countries. Some of them saw the news, commented on how awful it was for those poor people, said a prayer or two, and then stopped thinking about it.

"Others who saw the news not only prayed, but donated money to one of the international relief organizations that were bringing aid to the people of that poor nation. Then they went back to their lives, happy to have done something good.

"There were a few who wondered about the drought and why it was so devastating. They went online to learn more about it, and discovered that it was linked to climate change and that intense droughts were going to be an even greater problem in the decades ahead, especially impacting the world's poorest people. They learned about the causes of climate change, and came to realize that their own way of living was a major part of the problem. They hadn't known! They had simply lived as others did around them. At first this made them feel terribly guilty, but then, after a period of much prayer and questioning, they discovered that they, too, suffered from drought—an inner drought. And they become aware of a deep thirst: they thirsted for connectedness, for meaning, for love, for justice.

"This thirst opened their hearts and prompted them to action. They decided to simplify their lives for the sake of those suffering halfway around the world, as well as for the sake of future generations. Over time they found all sorts of ways to cut their own energy use; they also rediscovered the joy of spending time outdoors, reading, playing instruments, growing things and visiting, and they got more involved in the community. Some of them also donated money to relief organizations, and some of them didn't, but they all rediscovered the heart of their faith and their connectedness to the world around them. They were less distracted, less anxious, and more joyful. They were happy to live simply, so that others could simply live."

Jesus turned to the politician, and asked, "What do you think? Which of these kinds of people have become neighbors to those who are suffering?"

The politician responded, "Those who discovered their own inner thirst, and changed their lives for the sake of people they couldn't even see–those halfway around the world and those of the future."

Jesus said, "Go and do the same, and you will find freedom, love and joy."

David Backes has written and spoken on various aspects of the environment and the spiritual journey for many years. He teaches courses on these themes at the University of Wisconsin-Milwaukee, and is also ordained as a Roman Catholic deacon. He blogs at http://new-wood.blogspot.com.

TUESDAY

"Companions on the Journey"
Stan Thornburg

We're heading to Jerusalem. We do it every year. You'd think we would learn. We know what awaits us, i.e. betrayal and crucifixion, death and darkness, suffering of all kinds. Even so, we choose this journey with joy and passion, with deep gratitude and awe, with a profound sense of mystery that surpasses our ability to understand, and an awareness of that great sacrifice – that firestorm of unimaginable love – that works our redemption and brings us face to face with the terrible holiness of the divine.

Easter mornings we rush to the grave and again and again stare in wonder at the empty tomb. We stand, mouths agape at this feat of supernatural strength, fueled by unconditional love, accomplishing what all the sacrifices, piety, prayers, and incense could not even broach. Our heads want to burst as we try to piece it together into some coherent message. Our hearts in turn want to burst as we try to entertain even the smallest notion of the love we have just encountered. We stand helpless before it, we are unwitting victims of it, we can neither direct it nor control it though we try every theological parlor trick available to do so. Exhausted, we finally just let it go and allow it to be what it is…"For God so loved THE WORLD…"

"Oh God!" "Thank you for this awful and wonderful self-revelation."

We are not alone on this journey. We are accompanied by hundreds of thousands of believers from every corner of the globe. We are not just sojourners; we are brothers and sisters, joined in solidarity for this great celebration. There is no distinction. There is no room for labels, for doctrinal snobbery, for claims of exclusivity. There is only room for gratitude for one another and joy at being part of such a great throng. We are marching to the Holy Mountain where God resides and Christ reigns. Our hearts long for justice, for peace, for healing, for a glimpse of God's unconditional love lived out among us.
Is this the vision of which Isaiah wrote?

> "In the last days
> the mountain of the Lord's temple will be established
> as chief among the mountains;

it will be raised above the hills,
and all nations will stream to it.
Many peoples will come and say,
"Come, let us go up to the mountain of the LORD,
to the house of the God of Jacob.
He will teach us his ways,
so that we may walk in his paths."
The law will go out from Zion,
the word of the LORD from Jerusalem.
He will judge between the nations
and will settle disputes for many peoples.
They will beat their swords into plowshares
and their spears into pruning hooks.
Nation will not take up sword against nation,
nor will they train for war anymore.[52]

Everyone is invited on this journey! It belongs to no one faith or sect. We will weather the betrayal, suffering, and sacrifice together. Come, join the throngs across our globe on this wonderful, terrible, trek. We will stand stunned into silence before the tomb. We will go crazy with celebration when death's door makes way for resurrection power.

We will be forever changed.

✙

Stan Thornburg is a Quaker pastor at a small church in the Willamette Valley of western Oregon. He really loves ideas and is spiritually and intellectually hungry at all times. He finds his grounding in contemplative spiritual practices and in trusting the community. He blogs at born-to-eat-toast.blogspot.com.

Wednesday

"Small Steps"
Penny Carothers

To those from the West, Calcutta, India, assaults your senses and can steal your hope. Decaying buildings slant this way and that over lean-to dwellings that shelter families who have fled the countryside in hope of a better life. Like millions before the, they find little more than squalor.

At home it's easy to forget the desperation – both theirs and mine. In many ways, I must forget in order to go on. When I have the stomach to remember, I push back hopelessness. But I can't forget their faces.

Asa and Jebodah are sisters, about twelve and thirteen. Their father is gone and their mother provides for them by selling herself at the temple of Kali, goddess of destruction. They live on a mat on a four-lane street, a few blocks from Mother Theresa's Home for the Dying. They are covered in soot. They ask us for powder for their hair, and we buy it because they deserve to feel beautiful, if only for a day. Still, questions assault me constantly: How can I make a difference in a city that has so much need?

One day in Calcutta, a friend and I went out to distribute toys and clothing to the hungry and often hopeless children on the street. We stepped past the sewer and tentatively approached the lean-tos, our offerings in sweaty hands. And they came slowly at first. As they received their gifts, we saw delight in their faces and we smiled. But the moment lasted only seconds. Before we knew it, desperate hands had wrested our gifts from us, and in the violence of the moment we let go and fell back into the gutter. And I could think only of one thing: What have we accomplished, really?

In my disillusionment I saw them: Asa and Jebodah entered the filth to take our hands. They pulled us away and took us, dazed, to the water pump. And then they bent down and began to wash the grime off our feet. Beside me, my friend repeated over and over, "They are washing our feet."

Now back home, I have lost the urgency. I can ignore the people who sit on the sidewalks and the overpasses because the desperation is hidden, I don't have to engage it. I don't even have to know my neighbors. Some days, I remember

Calcutta's greatest lesson: I need my neighbors - these girls, these men I walk past with a nod – just as much as they need my help.

Today as I remember these girls, I remember my own need. I remember the beauty of their gift to us, but no less the incomprehensibility of their lives. On good days, I risk praying for the strength to step into the pain of the world with an open heart. Taking small steps, if need be, but moving – yes, into confusion and discomfort – but also moving toward them and toward hope.

Penny is 30-something writer and editor, among many other things. She is working on a memoir chronicling her mother's descent into mental illness and her attempts to make sense of it when she discovered Jesus in her twenties. She blogs at http://pennycarothers.com.

Maundy Thursday

"The Passover Meal"
Douglas Woods

Today, the fifteenth day of the month of Nisan, was Passover. It struck me as I went about my busy day today that just shy of 2000 years ago, Jesus died, but that for God, all time is now.

While I was busy getting my kids off to school, Jesus was busy staggering his cross to Calvary.

While I was busy at the store buying my bitter herbs, Jesus was busy being nailed to the cross.

While I was busy choosing the Seder wine, Jesus was rejecting the wine with gall.

While I went through my busy day, doing both good and evil, Jesus hung on the cross and took it all.

While the kids were packing up their school supplies, Jesus was commending his Mother to John.

While I was busy picking up the kids, Jesus was busy dying.

While I went about preparing our Seder Dinner, Joseph of Arimathea was negotiating for Jesus' body.

While our family celebrated our simple Seder dinner, Joseph and Nicodemus buried Jesus in the tomb.

While I was busy washing the dishes, the authorities were busy sealing His tomb.

It was a very busy day.

✢

Douglas Woods is a longtime friend and supporter of Mustard Seed Associates. He is especially passionate about the Mustard Seed Village project and lives in the Seattle area.

GOOD FRIDAY

"Washing Hands: A Reflection on Good Friday"
John Van de Laar

A Reflection for Good Friday on John 18:28-19:22

In my opinion one of the most powerful depictions of Pilate's encounter with Jesus is the scene from the 1973 movie *Jesus Christ Superstar*.[53]

Yes, there are liberties taken with the Gospel narrative, and there are some theological perspectives that I find unhelpful ("Everything is fixed and you can't change it..." for example), but the interplay between the two men, and Pilate's emotional turmoil is shown with rare energy and insight. As Jesus arrives in Pilate's court, the Governor meets him with the expected dismissiveness. "So, this is Jesus Christ. I am really quite surprised. You look so small. Not a king at all..." But, as the trial continues, after Jesus returns from Herod, Pilate becomes increasingly afraid and unsettled. What begins as another day at the office – find some pretext for the death sentence, sign the decree and move on to the next task – turns into a searching interaction in which the judge becomes the questioned and the victim becomes the (compassionate, even here) judge.

Finally, unable to find a reason to execute Jesus, certain that Christ is innocent but too scared to follow his conviction and risk loosing his power and his favour with Rome, Pilate simply hands him over to be crucified. He checks out and allows the people to do what they want with Jesus. In Matthew's Gospel (and in Jesus Christ Superstar) he even washes his hands to absolve himself of the responsibility.

I wonder if it worked. I wondered if he slept well that night, or if the knowledge of his collusion with the crowd plagued him. I wonder whether he was able to believe that he had no responsibility in the death of Jesus. I wonder if, in some way, his insistence that the sign above Jesus retain the words "Jesus of Nazareth, the King of the Jews" (John 19:19) was some small attempt to find redemption for himself. History, albeit sketchy, does seem to indicate that the death of Jesus haunted Pilate for a long time afterwards. One tradition has him committing suicide in remorse, while other, more reliable accounts indicate that Pilate was eventually recalled to Rome for the harsh and insensitive manner in which he treated the people under his rulership. Certainly, the history of faith has not let

Pilate off the hook so easily, and his hand washing has not freed him from being held responsible for Christ's death.

It would seem, strange, then, that people who claim the name of Christ would so easily follow Pilate's example. It's like Good Friday has become for some of us a giant bowl in which our hands can be washed clean of any and every destructive and selfish act we do. Back when I was an avid Survivor[54] fan, I was shocked when one of the contestants (who went on to win her season) laughed about the deception and broken promises she had employed to further herself in the game. After admitting to the camera (but no one else) what she had done, she shrugged and said, "I'll just ask Jesus to forgive me and it will be ok."

This attitude is all too prevalent in the Christian world. Rather than do the tough work of reflecting on our attitudes and actions, we simply do what we want, and, if people are hurt in the process, we wash our hands while claiming Christ's forgiveness. Rather than face the genuine and serious damage that our faith has done to minorities, women and people of other religions, we simply wash our hands and claim Christ's forgiveness. Rather than take responsibility for our brokenness and destructiveness – which would open us to the possibility of real transformation – we simply wash our hands and claim the forgiveness of Christ. It frightens me when Good Friday becomes the excuse which turns Christianity into an escape from responsibility and self-reflection.

This Holy Week I refuse to wash my hands. Rather, I will pray that God forces me to see whatever blood and dirt may be embedded in the cracks and lines of my skin. I will ask God to show me how I have contributed to the evil that continues to crucify innocent people on the altars of expediency, greed, power and self-righteousness. I will pray to be shown the places where I have colluded with corruption and where I have taken the easy way out. I will not try to save myself by working harder, but neither will I mindlessly dip my hands into the blood of Christ's sacrifice and believe that I need do no more to be "saved". Rather, I will ask God to burn the sight of the blood on my hands into my heart so that I am broken with the knowledge that I am part of the addictive system that kills the poor, the weak and the disconnected. And I will pray that the sight will lead me to tears, because only when I have taken responsibility for what is broken in me will I be able to receive the transformation – and embrace the pain of it – that God's grace and God's Spirit seek to work in me.

Lord, have mercy
Christ, have mercy
Lord, have mercy.

✛

John van de Laar is a Methodist minister and the founding director of Sacredise.com, a liturgical training and publishing ministry. He holds a Masters degree in Theology and is the author of The Hour That Changes Everything *and* Learning to Belong. *John lives in Cape Town, South Africa, with his wife Debbie (also a minister) and they have two sons.*

HOLY SATURDAY

"Summer Breaking"
Ryan Harrison

It happened eight years ago, but I can't stop thinking about it. One moment, melted into forever, into my eternity. It's become that which I look for in my life: that one breath, sigh of relief, of burdens being lifted and the true meaning of his words. "Come to me all you who are weary and heavy-laden, for my burden is easy and my yoke is light. Come to me, full of grief, of sorrow, of hopes unanswered. Come to me, full of anxiety, of pride, of an empty desire to control."

Eight years ago I sat on a beach in North Africa. It was hotter than hot and we sat– the foreigners and the locals alike, heavy with sweat and stiff muscles, the way we craned our necks to reach out to the breeze that wasn't there.

Children tucked in at their mother's feet not daring to run to the water's edge– too hot anyway for jolly. The birds would flitter across the slow, short waves, the waves themselves too tired to roll.

And then it happened. Slowly the hair on the back of our necks lifted, unmatted from the skin. Women's veils, the ones with fringe on the end, started to tussle.

The breeze. Summer's chains clanging against fall's relief; summer breaking. That's what they call it.

When a season breaks, everything right in the world matters ten thousand times more than everything wrong. The children stretch, cool wind breathing life into their lungs, and they shout for joy, for the hope that is the breeze–no longer stranger, but friend.

Women start to laugh again. These sometimes women, sometimes product to be used, purchased for a time being and worn hard– they have life coursing through their veins again. Tomorrow seems closer, seems sweeter and softer than ever before. They lay back and float on the sand, their bodies light with the expectancy of a birth easier than they have ever known.

Tomorrow is sweet, but the shadows on the horizon dance, a harbinger of the coming pain. The next day? Not as sweet. Heavy. Sticky with pain. A cruel desert.

But again, God will bring the wind. He leads us out of our deserts, our skins hardened and wind-blasted. The wind polishes away the sand, the weight of the heat. He breaks them, those chains of ours. Those seasons of never-ending heavy grief.

And so we follow, through the desert.

Ryan Harrison lives in Denver, Colorado but her heart is in Morocco. She fills her days with reading, teaching, and ministering in the city. This reflection was first published on How We Spend Our Days at http://howwespendourdays.wordpress.com.

EASTER SUNDAY

"Easter Sunday"
Andy Wade

God smacked me upside the head with an amazing double rainbow the other day. The colors were so intense in one of the arcs that I could easily distinguish the many bands of color painted across the sky. I had to stop. I had to just stand there in awe and take it in.

This was a resurrection moment!

Penetrating our lives with joy, beauty and newness, resurrection moments are all around us every day. You don't plan them. You can't control them. You can only stop and enjoy them when they appear in your life.

But how many resurrection moments do we pass by each day, our vision clouded by busyness, distractions, or perhaps more likely, by being pre-conditioned not to notice them?

For me, the garden is a great place to train my eyes, heart, and mind to discover resurrection all around me. There are, of course, the obvious ones; planted seeds that germinate and burst through the soil, perennials that spring back to life each year, or one of my favorites, the early-blooming *Lenten Rose* proclaiming that winter is nearly over and spring is on its way. Like a rainbow in the sky, these signs of resurrection are difficult to miss.

But what about other signs of life, for example, the lowly dandelion? We North Americans spend millions of dollars on toxins to rid our yards of these invasive "weeds." (The United States spends more annually on lawn care than on foreign aid!) Yet these "weeds" are the most nutritious plants in the yard and provide some of the earliest flowers for bees to begin their spring ministry of pollination.

We have been sold an anti-dandelion worldview and miss the gift they can be to our gardens and our bodies. Not only that, but because we've unquestionably bought into this worldview, we spray and broadcast toxins that affect all of creation, right down to the hormones in our own bodies. We think that by ridding ourselves of these pesky "weeds" we're creating something beautiful when, in fact, we've only created a cheap imitation of paradise – all nice and shiny on the outside but, just under the surface, full of anti-resurrection power. And why? Because we've missed a resurrection moment.

As my wife and I plan the garden, planning splashes of texture and color in all the "right places," our frustration with squirrels rearranging our flower bulbs turns into an adventure. At first I was annoyed by them. "How can I stop these cute rats from messing up our plans?" But then God performed spiritual cataract surgery on the eyes of my heart. Suddenly I discovered joy in the random beauty as flowers started popping up all over in unexpected places. I don't need to attempt to control resurrection, just enter into it where it happens, give thanks, and enjoy it.

In a similar way, those raspberry shoots coming up in my path and wandering from my nice neat rows, and the borrage plants that are self-seeding throughout the garden, become not an annoyance, but rather an opportunity to share God's surprising resurrection moments with neighborhood friends and family.

You cannot control resurrection. You can reject it, ignore it, or embrace it – but you cannot control it.

Stepping out of the garden and into the neighborhood, there's Kevin. Society labeled him as "developmentally disabled." I used to see him that way too. But as I've gotten to know him over the years I've discovered the amazing, yet often hidden, gift he is to our community. Do you need to know or understand the relational connections in the church? Ask Kevin, he's a human database of knowledge. One day, as I was driving into town, he and a friend were at the crosswalk waiting to cross the street. The cars just kept passing him by. I stopped to let them cross, waved at him, and was greeted with shouts of approval! "That's Andy Wade! Andy Wade! Thanks, Andy Wade!" I felt like a rock star!

I see Kevin every morning as I take my son to school. We wave and smile. I'm moved inside. It's not that I'm something special because I'm friendly to Kevin. I'm someone special because Kevin is in my life. His wave, his smile, stirs up resurrection hope in my heart and brightens my day. It's amazing how quickly my mood can change with a simple smile and wave from him. I'm so glad not to have passed him by. Kevin helps me to see resurrection and makes me wonder if we've gotten those labels backward; perhaps it's those who pass by without noticing the joyful gift of people we've marginalized who are truly "developmentally disabled."

I'll confess, I miss way too many of the resurrections going on around me every day. I get busy, distracted, and overwhelmed with life. I forget that life itself is a daily resurrection. I hit the pillow after an exhausting day, and all the while God continues to breathe life into me and into all creation.

I rest.

God sustains.

Rising in the morning, if I take a moment to see, I discover God inviting me into a new day, a day God has already been at work preparing for me to walk into. The power of the resurrection of Jesus we celebrate on Easter Day is the same power at work in my own life and in the community and world around me.

God's transforming power can be seen in something as small as a dandelion and experienced in a most profound way when we allow God to tweak our perspectives, correct our vision, and resurrect relationships that are stuck in pre-resurrection, or even anti-resurrection, habits and attitudes.

When the double rainbow appeared in the sky I was driving. I was amazed, awed, grateful. I pulled over as soon as I could, but by that time one of the rainbows had vanished. I wonder how many resurrection moments I trample under foot because my vision is clouded and I'm speed-walking through life.

Yes, I am broken. But the good news is that God is a God of resurrection! Resurrection moments are happening all around us, every day. When we begin to realize this, slow down and take it in, that's when we also begin to see those resurrection-moments taking place in the soil of our own hearts, and we discover that we ourselves have become a resurrection moment.

Andy is a team member of Mustard Seed Associates and is an ordained Mennonite Pastor who has ministered in Seattle and Hong Kong and now lives with his family in Hood River, Oregon. When not working on MSA projects, Andy can be found working in the family's organic garden, hunting wild mushrooms, taking pictures, coordinating volunteers for the Hood River Warming Shelter, or just relaxing in the beauty of the Columbia River Gorge.

A LITANY FOR EASTER

Hold your head high, Christ has risen!
Rejoice and shout,
Christ has come, calling us home.
Home to the heart of God,
Home to God's living presence,
Home to God's banquet feast.

Hold your head high, Christ has risen!
Death has been conquered, suffering vanquished;
Christ has come, calling us home.
He is renewing and restoring us.
All that was broken is being made whole.
All that was dislocated is being set right.

Hold your head high, Christ has risen!
Now we see him,
In the faces of the poor,
In the hurting of the sick,
In the anguish of the oppressed.
Christ has come calling us home.

Hold your head high, Christ has risen!
Now we see him.
In the weakness of the vulnerable,
In the questions of the doubting,
In the fears of the dying.
Christ has come calling us home.

Hold your head high, Christ has risen!
In the celebration of the saints,
In the generosity of the faithful,
In the compassion of the caring.

Hold your head high, Christ has risen!
He transforms our world with love and hope,
He ignites our hearts of stone with compassion and care,
He transfigures our world with the spirit of life.

Hallelujah, Jesus Christ has risen and we see him!
Carry forward God's healing,
Christ has come, calling us home,
To a world where truth and justice triumph,
To a place where abundance flourishes,
To a community where generosity abounds.

Hold your head high, Christ has risen!
Christ has come, calling us home.
Our redemption is complete,
God's eternal world has begun.
Love reigns over all,
Hallelujah, Hallelujah, Hallelujah,
Christ has risen indeed!

APPENDICES

APPENDIX I: THE MUTUNGA CHALLENGE

The Mutunga $2 Challenge has captured people's imaginations, and many have accepted the challenge to restrict their food budget to $2 per person per day for a week. For many in our world, living on $2 per day is not a choice but a necessity. When speaking with Donna Carter in Calgary, Canada, about it, she shared a conversation she had with Ephraim Lindor, a pastor in Haiti where most people live on $1 per day. "Is that enough to live on?" She asked. "No!" he responded, "but it is enough not to die."

We are grateful for those who have accepted this challenge to identify with sisters and brothers who have so little and grapple with how to cut their food budget for a week in order to identify with and help those less fortunate than themselves. Here are some suggestions on how to proceed:

1. Make sure that everyone in the family participates in the negotiations revolving around how to spend your week's budget.

2. Discuss the sacrifices you will need to make and reflect on how to construct a suitable menu. Obviously we will all need to give up expensive food options like dining out, buying prepared and packaged meals, and lattes. Fruit juice, milk, and other beverages may need to be restricted, but then we all need to drink more water anyway. We may also need to give up time that we usually use for other activities in order to have time to cook meals from scratch.

3. Construct a menu and develop a budget for the whole week before you go shopping.

4. Estimate the value of food you already have in your cupboard that you plan to use during the week and subtract that from your week's budget. The only food that does not need to be included in your budget is fruit and vegetables that you have grown yourself. One of the reasons that rural poverty is often not as devastating nutritionally as urban poverty is because people are able to grow some of their own food to supplement what they need to buy.

Guidelines for Developing a Menu and Shopping List

Here are a few guidelines that will help you plan your menu:

1. Plan the budget based on $0.25 to $0.40 for breakfast, $0.50 to $0.75 for lunch and snacks, and $1.00 for dinner per person. Estimated values in recipes are based on Seattle prices 2012.

2. Prepared meals and processed food is always more expensive than basic staples like rice, potatoes, pasta, legumes, and beans. Bulk staples of rice, barley, oats, and bulgur wheat are less expensive than packaged versions. Find the bulk food section in your local supermarket or visit Whole Foods or an equivalent health food store.

3. Whole grains provide more protein and nutritional value than processed grains. Discover varieties you have never used before, like quinoa, couscous, and bulgur wheat.

4. Fruit and vegetables are usually cheapest at your local fruit market or Asian grocery.

5. Meat is probably one of the most expensive food items. Eating vegetarian meals or meals with very little meat will decrease your food budget considerably.

6. Eating fruit and vegetables that are in season and grown locally will be cheaper than those that are out of season or grown in distant places.

7. Leave space in your food budget for a special treat (especially if you have young children). You may like to make some inexpensive cookies at the beginning of the week.

8. Buy the generic brands. No more buying a brand name because it looks nice.

9. Buy in bulk and share meals with friends. Things like potatoes and onions are much cheaper when purchased in a very large bag. This is also true of things like salsa.

10. Lots of starch. Raw starch seems to be the cheapest type of food, like beans, flour, rice, and potatoes.

Suggested Recipes

Fish Cakes (serves 4)

    1 tin of tuna
    7 medium potatoes, mashed
    Breadcrumbs (made from bread supply for the week)
    2 onions, chopped
    2 eggs

Mash it all together. Form into small patties and then roll them in breadcrumbs. Cook in olive oil until golden brown both sides. Serve with fresh salad. If you grow your own herbs, add these too.

Recipe Total Cost[55]: $3.50
Per Serving Cost: $0.85

Vegetarian Autumn Garden Soup (serves 15)

    1 cup dried beans (use Scarlet Runners from the garden or large lima beans)
    1 cup wheat berries
    1 cup chopped onion
    4 cloves garlic, minced
    2 Tbsp olive oil
    1 Tbsp fresh sage, chopped
    1 lb fresh tomatoes, chopped, or 14 oz canned tomatoes, diced
    1 Tbsp fresh rosemary, chopped
    1 cup carrot, peeled and cut in ½-inch chunks
    1 lb cabbage, coarsely chopped
    ½ lb green beans, trimmed and cut into ½-inch lengths
    ¼ cup fresh parsley, chopped
    1 tsp salt
    ground pepper to taste
    6 cups vegetable broth
    1 cup winter squash, chopped
    ½ cup mushrooms, chopped

Soak beans and wheat berries in separate bowls overnight. Drain and set aside. Cook dried beans until just tender (45 min – 1 hour).

In a large pot or Dutch oven, heat olive oil over medium heat. Add onion and cook, stirring until soft. Add garlic, sage, and rosemary and stir until fragrant, about 1 minute. Add soaked wheat berries, tomatoes, broth, and water. Bring to a simmer, cover and cook until wheat berries are al dente (1 – 1½ hours). Add cabbage, squash, mushrooms, carrots, green beans, and soaked beans with their liquid. Cover and simmer until all vegetables are tender (15 – 20 minutes). Stir in parsley and season with salt and pepper.

This soup can be adapted to take advantage of whatever vegetables are most plentiful.

Recipe Total Cost: $10.00
Per Serving Cost: $0.65

Phad Thai (serves 5)

1 lb medium rice noodles
2 Tbsp vegetable oil
3 eggs, beaten
2 cups fresh bean sprouts
1 bunch green onions, chopped
1 clove garlic, crushed
½ tsp fish sauce
¼ cup dry roasted peanuts, chopped
Parsley or cilantro

Bring water to a boil. Add noodles and remove from heat. Let sit for 3 minutes, drain, and set aside. Heat half the vegetable oil in a wok or frying pan. Pour in eggs and cook until firm. Don't stir. Remove from pan and cut in thin strips. Set aside.

Sauté garlic, scallions, and bean sprouts in the rest of the vegetable oil. Add fish and oyster sauces and mix well. Add drained noodles and mix again. Add strips of egg and mix. Put on a serving plate and garnish with chopped peanuts, parsley, or cilantro, and if desired, cooked shrimp.

Recipe Total Cost: $3.50
Per Serving Cost: $0.70

PEA AND HAM SOUP (SERVES 15)

    500g borlotti beans (or any other split peas/beans that are cheap)
    1 clove garlic, minced
    1 onion, diced
    2 stalks celery, chopped
    Salt and pepper to taste
    1 tsp cumin
    1 tsp Italian herb mix
    375g frozen peas
    5 medium potatoes, diced
    6 carrots, diced
    1 ham hock

Soak beans overnight. Sauté garlic, onion, celery, and herbs in a little margarine or butter. Add ham hock, beans, remaining vegetables, and enough water to make a thick soup. Simmer until vegetable are soft and meat falls away from bones.

Recipe Total Cost: $7.50
Per Serving Cost: $0.50

VEGAN MOROCCAN COUSCOUS (SERVES 8)

    1 cup dried garbanzo beans
    1 Tbsp olive oil
    1 onion, diced
    3 cups vegetable broth
    2 carrots, peeled and diced
    2 turnips, peeled and diced
    1 sweet potato, diced
    1 zucchini, diced
    1 red bell pepper, diced
    1 15-oz can tomato sauce
    ¼ tsp ground cinnamon
    ½ tsp ground turmeric
    1 pinch curry powder
    2 cups uncooked couscous

Soak garbanzo beans overnight and cook.

Heat oil in a large pot over medium-high heat; sauté onion until golden. Pour in vegetable broth and bring to a boil. Stir in carrots, turnips, and sweet potato. Reduce heat to medium and simmer 15 minutes. Reduce heat to low and add zucchini and red bell pepper. Simmer for 20 minutes.

Stir in cooked garbanzo beans, tomato sauce, cinnamon, turmeric, and curry powder. Simmer until heated through. Meanwhile, bring 2½ cups water to a boil. Stir in couscous, cover, and remove from heat. Let stand 5 to 7 minutes. Fluff with a fork and serve with vegetables on top.

Recipe Total Cost: $9.00
Per Serving Cost: $1.10

Rice and Beans Burritos (serves 4)

4 10-inch tortillas
1 cup uncooked rice
1 cup dried black beans
1 onion, diced
1 clove garlic, minced
1 tsp oregano
1 tsp cumin
1 4-oz can mild green chilies
¼ cup salsa
4 Tbsp sour cream

Soak beans in overnight. Boil for 1 – 1½ hours or until soft. Set aside. Cook rice. Sauté onions in 1 tablespoon olive oil, add garlic, oregano, chopped green chilies, and cooked beans. Divide into 4 parts. Spoon over tortillas. Add salsa and sour cream. Roll up.

Recipe Total Cost: $4.00
Per Serving Cost: $1.00

CARROT CAKE

    2 eggs
    ½ cup sugar
    ½ cup oil
    1 cup whole wheat flour
    ½ tsp baking soda
    1 tsp allspice
    ½ cup carrot, grated

Whisk together eggs, sugar, and oil. Sift flour, baking soda, and allspice. Combine wet and dry ingredients with carrots. Mix well. Bake in greased loaf tin in moderate oven for 50 min.

Recipe Total Cost: $2.00
Per Serving Cost: $0.35

APPENDIX II: ADDITIONAL RESOURCES

We hope that your journey of discovery has deepened your relationship to God, to God's people, and to God's world. Through confronting our own brokenness we find the healing God desires for us and are enabled to become God's loving hands of compassion and care in a world that desperately needs healing. We hope this study has prompted permanent changes in your life that will lead you into new journeys of discovery. The following resources may help you continue your journey.

BOOKS

- Judy Bauer, compiler. *Lent and Easter: Wisdom from Henri J.M. Nouwen* (Ligouri, MO: Liguori Publications, 2005).
- Lynne M. Baab, *Fasting: Spiritual Freedom Beyond Our Appetites.* (Downer's Grove, IL: InterVarsity Press, 2006).
- John Bunyan. *Pilgrim's Progress,* Revised Edition (UK: Penguin Classics, 2009).
- Phillis Tickle, *The Shaping of a Life: A Spiritual Landscape* (Colorado Springs, CO: Image Books, 2003).
- Paul Elie, *The Life You Save May Be Your Own: An American Pilgrimage* (New York: Farrar, Straus and Giroux, 2003).
- Richard Foster, *The Celebration of Discipline: The Path to Spiritual Growth* (New York: HarperCollins, 1998).
- Brother Victor-Antoine d'Avila-Latourrette, *A Monastic Year: Reflections from a Monastery* (Dallas, TX: Taylor Trade Publishing, 1996).
- Brother Victor-Antoine d'Avila-Latourette, *Twelve Months of Monastery Soups* (New York, NY: Broadway Books, 1998)
- Christine Sine, *GodSpace: Time for Peace in the Rhythms of Life* (San Francisco, CA: Barclay, 2006).
- Christine Sine, *Return to Our Senses: Reimagining How We Pray* (Seattle, WA: MSA Publications, 2013).
- Lauren Winner, *Girl Meets God: On the Path to a Spiritual Life* (New York: Algonquin Books, 2002).
- Joan Chittister, *The Liturgical Year: The Spiraling Adventure of the Spiritual Life* (Nashville, TN: Thomas Nelson, 2009)
- Marjorie Thompson, *Soul Feast* (Westminster John Knox Press; Reprinted 2005)
- Ann Voskamp, *A Thousand Gifts: A Dare to Live Fully Right Where You Are* (New York: HarperCollins Publishing, 2011)

- Christine Valters Paintner, *Desert Fathers and Mothers: Early Christian Wisdom Sayings* (Woodstock, VT: Skylight Paths Publishing, 2012)
- Julie Clawson, *Everyday Justice: The Global Impact of Our Daily Choices* (Downer's Grove, IL: IVP Books, 2009).

WEBSITES

DAILY SCRIPTURE READINGS AND MEDITATIONS

- Additional daily reflections, prayers, video meditations and podcasts on Christine Sine's blog: http://godspace-msa.com
- The Daily Office: http://www.missionstclare.com/english/ (from the Book of Common Prayer and the New Zealand Prayer Book)
- Presbyterian USA daily readings: www.presbyterianmission.org/devotion/daily/2013/10/28/
- Northumbria Community Daily Offices: www.northumbriacommunity.org/offices/how-to-use-daily-office/
- Daily Prayer with the Irish Jesuits: http://www.sacredspace.ie/
- Daily Prayer from the Catholic Church in Australia: http://www.catholicaustralia.com.au/page.php?pg=prayer-index
- Reflections from Forward Day by Day: http://prayer.forwardmovement.org/forward_day_by_day.php?d=28&m=10&y=2013

RESOURCES FOR READINGS FOR THE ENTIRE YEAR

- The Voice: The entire liturgical calendar of readings from the revised common lectionary. http://www.crivoice.org/daily.html
- Christianity: This site provides various plans for reading the entire Bible in a year: http://www.biblestudytools.com/bible-reading-plan/
- Upper Room Ministries provides beautiful and often very moving daily devotional prayers and meditations. http://devotional.upperroom.org/

RESOURCES FOR PRAYING FOR THE VULNERABLE AND HUNGRY DURING LENT

- ELCA has a great World Hunger Lenten Series available with lots of good information and suggestions. They go for a $3/day diet – probably more doable today then the $2/day we have always attempted. It can be found at: http://www.uss-elca.org/for-congregations/world-hunger/2011-world-hunger-lenten-series.

- Bread for the World always produces wonderful resources for Lent each year that challenge us to face the issues of hunger. In 2013 they worked in collaboration with Women of Faith for the 1,000 Days Movement to develop a series of Lenten activities around the theme of Maternal and Child Nutrition in the 1,000 day window between pregnancy and a child's second birthday. Lent-specific resources can be found at: http://www.bread.org/help/church/worship/lent/. Information can be found at http://www.bread.org/hunger/maternal-child-nutrition/women-of-faith-for-the-1000.html
- Episcopal Relief and Development chose the alleviation of hunger to be the theme of their Lenten Meditations in 2013 too. They are available in both English and Spanish and can be downloaded for free at http://www.episcopalrelief.org/church-in-action/church-campaigns/lent.
- Presbyterian Hunger program produces great resources on food justice including this Lenten guide http://www.pcusa.org/resource/lenten-fast-insight-action-gospel-john-presbyteria/

Facts, Statistics and Challenges on Hunger, Poverty and Environmental Issues

- United Nations Development Program: http://www.undp.org
- United Nations World Food Program: http://www.wfp.org
- UN-HABITAT: http://www.unhabitat.org
- The Mutunga $2 Challenge, http://www.mutunga.com
- The Two Dollar Challenge: http://www.twodollarchallenge.org
- 100-Mile Diet, http://100milediet.org
- The Global Footprint Network: http://www.footprintnetwork.org
- Eco-footprint quiz: http://ecofoot.org/
- Archbishop Thabo Magkoba, convener of the Anglican Environmental Network in South Africa, called for the church to undertake a Carbon Fast during Lent 2013. His recommendations can be found at http://acen.anglicancommunion.org/_userfiles/File/a_carbon_fast_for_lent.pdflivepage.apple.com.
- Additional helpful suggestions and external resources about how to undertake a carbon fast can be found at The Oil Lamp's website, http://www.theoillamp.co.uk/?p=1520.

Resources for Holy Week

- Textweek.com has an excellent and very comprehensive list of resources for Lent and Holy week.

- Faith at Home has great children's activities for each day of Holy week: http://www.faith-at-home.com/tips/holy-week.html.

For Palm Sunday

- Little Takas has colouring pages available for Palm Sunday at http://www.littletaka.com/2010/03/22/kids-activity-sheets-palm-sunday-the-triumphal-entry/
- If you want to learn to make Palm Sunday crosses, watch this YouTube video: http://www.youtube.com/watch?v=oXnEdYSAvtQ

For Maundy Thursday

- This post contains a number of suggestions for Maundy Thursday (updated annually): http://godspace-msa.com/2013/03/21/resources-for-holy-week-2013-maundy-thursday

For Good Friday

From New Zealand :

- This series of Stations of the Cross comes from Hamilton New Zealand. It includes a link to a good explanation of stations of the Cross http://www.stations.org.nz/about/images/
- Cityside Baptist church in Auckland New Zealand has held an exhibit of contemporary icons to reflect on at Easter for a number of years. Several of their presentations can be viewed on line including this one entitled Desert Files http://cityside.org.nz/projects-events/desertfiles

From the Middle East and Sudan:

- A heartrending presentation of the stations of the Cross using images of refugees from Iraq and Sudan as spectators and participants from St Pauls Norwalk CT (The stations of the Cross are down the side of the post) http://www.prweb.com/releases/2005/08/prweb274092.htm
- An interesting set of Jordanian stamps which Mansour Mouasher found depicting the Stations of the Cross http://www.pbase.com/mansour_mouasher/stations_of_the_cross

From South America:

- A very powerful presentation of the stations from the perspective of liberation theology by Adolfo Pérez Esquivel of Argentina http://www.alastairmcintosh.com/general/1992-stations-cross-esquivel.pdf

From Asia:

- I enjoyed meditating on this series with meditations by the Most Reverend Thomas Menamparampil Archbishop of Guwahati India. http://www.vatican.va/news_services/liturgy/2009/documents/ns_lit_doc_20090410_via-crucis_en.html
- A very beautiful Korean Stations of the Cross from Myeong-dong Cathedral by Korean sculptor Choi Jong-tae. http://www.flickr.com/photos/68558939@N00/3158658815/in/photostream/

From Africa:

- From Hekima College, Nairobi, Kenya. The designs were created by Father Angelbert M. Vang SJ from Yaoude, from the Cameroon who was a well-known historian, poet, musician and designer and executed by a Kenyan artist. http://www.sjweb.info/world/stations/index.cfm
- This meditation is a poignant reminder of those who struggle daily to carry crosses we cannot even imagine.

From the U.K.:

- This Stations of the Cross series by Chris Gollon was commissioned by the Church of England for the Church of St John on Bethnal Green, in East London. Gollon took the unusual step of using his own son as the model for Jesus, his daughter as Mary, and his wife as Veronica. Fr Alan Green is cast as Nicodemus, and David Tregunna (Gollon's friend and agent) as Joseph of Arimathea. The juxtaposition of real figures with imagined ones creates a heightened sense of reality. I think that the images are both compelling and powerful. They can be found at http://www.chrisgollon.com/collections/stations-of-the-cross/

VIDEOS (FROM YOUTUBE)

- A powerful presentation produced by Jesuit Brother Edward Sheehy of the passion story: http://www.youtube.com/watch?v=HwkznTGOFAc
- A poignant presentation and reminder of those who carry their crosses daily through their suffering: http://www.youtube.com/watch?v=MsDFJicDkmw
- A mimed rendition From Netherlands of Sandy Patti's "Via Dolorosa" can be found at http://www.youtube.com/watch?v=31urACOSS1o.

ENDNOTES

1 Theresa Froehlich, Life Coach, February 17, 2012, http://www.transitionslifecoaching.org/2012/02/3177/ (accessed January 2, 2014).

2 Judy Bauer comp. *Lent and Easter Wisdom from Henri Nouwen* (Ligouri, Mis.: Ligouri Press, 2005), 4.

3 Thomas Merton, *Seasons of Celebration: Meditations on the Cycle of Liturgical Feasts* (Notre Dame, IN: Ave Maria Press, 2000), 13.

4 Dorothy C. Bass, "Keeping Sabbath" in *Practicing our Faith: A Way of Life for a Searching People*, ed. Dorothy C Bass (San Francisco, CA: Jossey-Bass, 2010), 75.

5 The index of weekly lectionary readings and additional resources for the liturgical year can be accessed online at http://crivoice.org/index.html.

6 "The Challenge of the Lenten Season: Evangelical Protestants are Caught between Freedom in Christ and Sacred Observance," *Christianity Today,* March 14, 1960. http://www.christianitytoday.com/ct/2000/marchweb-only/33.0.html. Republished in the *CT Ediorial Archives* on March 1, 2000 (accessed Feburary 20, 2012).

7 "Beyond Bunnies: The Real Meaning of Easter Season," narr. Michelle Norris, All Things Considered, National Public Radio, April 18, 2011. This broadcast can be found online at http://www.npr.org/2011/04/18/135517274/beyond-bunnies-the-real-meaning-of-easter-season (accessed January 2, 2014).

8 Andrew Santella, "Get Lent: Protestants do the Sober Season," http://www.slate.com/articles/life/faithbased/2006/02/get_lent.html (accessed January 2, 2014).

9Quote taken from Lauren Winner's article "Giving Up Sex for Lent: My Friends' Fast from Sex Gets to the Heart of Lenten Discipline." The article can be found at http://www.beliefnet.com/Faiths/Christianity/Lent/Giving-Up-Sex-For-Lent.aspx (accessed January 2, 2014).

10 Taken from"Beyond Bunnies: Th Real Meaning of Easter Season," NPR interview with Michelle Norris (April 18, 2011).

11 Brian Doerksen, Return to Me, "Holy God," Integrity Music. CD. 2007.

12 To clarify for American readers: "take-away" is the English term for take-out food.

13 Rev. Tim Phillips is the Lead Pastor at Seattle First Baptist Church.

14George MacDonald, *Thomas Wingfold Curate*, Vol. 3, (Resounding Wind Publishing, 2012), NOOK edition, p. 338.

15 John 15:5, TNIV.

16 Gertrude Mueller Nelson, *To Dance with God* (Mahwah, NJ: Paulist Press), 129.

17More information can be found at http://www.mutunga.com. The Mutunga $2 Challenge is a trademark of the Mutunga Partnership.

18 Visit http://www.twodollarchallenge.org for more information.

19 Franklin D. Roosevelt, "Second Inaugural Address," January 10, 1937, accessed February 3, 2009, at http://www.bartleby.com/124/pres50.html.

20 Anup Shah, "Poverty Facts and Stats," on *Global Issues: Social, Political, Economic, and Environmental Issues that Affect Us All.* http://www.globalissues.org/article/26/poverty-facts-and-stats (accessed Oct 8, 2013).

21 H. Luke Shaefer and Kathryn Edin, "Extreme Poverty in the United States, 1996-2012," National Poverty Center Policy Brief 24 (2008), http://npc.umich.edu/publications/policy_briefs/brief28/policybrief28.pdf, accessed October 8, 2013.

22 Michelle Castillo, "U.S. has highest first day infant mortality out of industrialized world, group reports," http://www.cbsnews.com/8301-204_162-57583237/u.s-has-highest-first-day-infant-mortality-out-of-industrialized-world-group-reports/(accessed October 8, 2013).

23 Robert Bryce. "Feed a person for a year or fill up an SUV," http://www.alternet.org/story/48790/ethanol%3A_feed_a_person_for_a_year_or_fill_up_an_suv

24 Joan Chittister, *The Liturgical Year* (Nashville, Tennessee, Thomas Nelson, 2009) 105.

25 ibid Chittister, p. 104

26 ibid Chittister, p. 105

27 Zephaniah 3:17.

28 An organization called One Day's Wages empowers individuals and groups to "birthday for a cause" that supports the eradication of global poverty (such as the provision of clean water, health care, school tuition, etc.). More information can be found at their website (http://onedayswages.org/birthday).

29 Miguel de Cervantes Saavedra, *Don Quixote de la Mancha*, trans. by Edith Grossman (Harper Perennial, 2005).

30 UN-HABITAT, UN-HABITAT's strategy for the implementation of the Millennium Development Goal 7 target 11, 2005, accessed February 3, 2009, at http://www.unhabitat.org/pmss/getPage.asp?page=bookView&book=1805.

31 Ibid., 7.

32 Real Change is available in Seattle, WA. More information can be found at www.realchangenews.org. See if there is something similar in your neighbourhood.

33 http://www.homepdx.net

34http://www.drybonesdenver.org/

35 http://www.cartsvictoria.ca

36 "Learn More about the 100 Mile Diet" can be found at http://www.learnstuff.com/learn-about-the-100-mile-diet/.

37 Romans 8:18 – 25, Phillips Translation.

38 Jn 12:24, New Living Translation.

39 Is 45:8, NLT

40 Rev 21:5; 22:2, NLT.

41 One place that this lament took place was during the Duke Center for Reconciliation's 2010 Summer Institute. A piece written at the beginning of the Institute is entitled, "The BP Oil Spill: A Christian Call for Lament and Reconciliation." It can be found at http://sustainabletraditions.com/2010/06/the-bp-oil-spill-a-christian-call-for-lament-and-reconciliation/

42 Nancy Ortberg, *Looking for God: An Unexpected Journey through Tattoos, Tofu, and Pronouns* (Carol Stream, IL: Tyndale House, 2008), 16.

43 Jin S Kim, "A Pentecostal Vision for the Church," Presbyterians for Renewal website, March 2, 2003, accessed February 3, 2009, at https://www.pfrenewal.org/issues/234-a-pentecostal-vision-for-the-church.

44 James 2:8, Today's New International Version.

45 Barbara Ehrenreich, *Nickel and Dimed: On (Not) Getting By in America.* New York: Metropolitan Books, 2001.

46 Ranya Idliby and Suzanne Oliver and Priscilla Warner, *The Faith Club: A Muslim, A Christian, a Jew—Three Women Searching for Understanding*, Atria Books, 2007.

47 Taken from the accolades listed at the beginning of *The Faith Club*.

48 Joan D. Chittister, *Called to Question: A Spiritual Memoir* (Sheed & Ward, 2004), 14.

49 Stated by Kathryn Hepburn's character in the film, The Lion in Winter (UK: Avco Emory Pictures, 1968).

50 Matthew 21:9, TNIV.

51 Matthew 21:9, NIV.

52 Micah 4:2-3.

53 Jesus Christ Superstar, directed by Norman Jewison (United Kingdom: Universal Studios, 1973), VHS.

54 Survivor is a reality TV series that has aired in the United States from 2000 to the present. Created and produced by Charlie Parsons.

55 Price estimations based on 2012 food costs in Seattle, WA.

Made in the USA
Charleston, SC
30 January 2014